THE
WESTERN BATTLEFIELDS

Official Photograph.] *Frontispiece.*

Marshal Joffre.　President Poincaré.　H.M. The King.　Marshal Foch.　Field-Marshal Lord Haig.
THE VICTORY SMILE.

Published by

The Naval & Military Press Ltd
Unit 5 Riverside, Brambleside
Bellbrook Industrial Estate
Uckfield, East Sussex
TN22 1QQ England

Tel: +44 (0)1825 749494

www.naval-military-press.com
www.nmarchive.com

In reprinting in facsimile from the original, any imperfections are inevitably reproduced and the quality may fall short of modern type and cartographic standards.

THE WESTERN BATTLEFIELDS

A GUIDE TO THE BRITISH LINE

SHORT ACCOUNT OF THE FIGHTING
THE TRENCHES & POSITIONS

By
Lieut.-Col. T. A. LOWE, D.S.O., M.C.
The Royal Irish Regiment
(Late Comdg. 1st Bn. The Royal Irish Fusiliers)

The Naval & Military Press Ltd

THE TOURS DESCRIBED IN THIS BOOK CAN ONLY BE CARRIED OUT COMFORTABLY BY MOTOR CAR.

■ ■ ■

WE provide Private Motor Cars with Officer Guides who have fought over the actual ground, and make all arrangements for Hotel accommodation, etc., in advance from London.

PRIVATE VISITS BY CAR
—— TO WAR GRAVES ——

■ ■ ■

Imperial Travel Bureau (Association of Ex-Officers) **LTD.**

132 SLOANE STREET, LONDON, S.W. 1

Tel. Victoria 1074

CONTENTS

	PAGE
INTRODUCTION...	ix

CHAPTER I
Preliminary Plans—Walking the Best Method of Progress—What to Wear—What to Take—What to Avoid.   1

CHAPTER II
The Journey from England—Folkestone to Boulogne, the Main Artery of Communications during the War—Other Routes—A Day in Boulogne—The Plan of the Book   5

CHAPTER III
The "Key" Towns: Poperinghe, the Key to Flanders—Lille, the Key to Ploegsteert Wood, Armentieres, and Givenchy—St. Pol, the Key to La Bassee, Lens, Loos, and Vimy—Doullens, The Key to Arras—Amiens, the Key to the Somme   11

CHAPTER IV
Daily Trips from Poperinghe: A Visit to the Yser Canal—Pilkem and St. Julien—A Day at Hooge and Gheluvelt — Kemmel, Wytschaete, and the Messines Ridge—How to reach Passchendaele   18

CHAPTER V
Daily Trips from Lille: Armentieres—Ploegsteert Wood — Neuve Chapelle — Festubert and Givenchy   26

CHAPTER VI
Daily Trips from St. Pol: Loos—The Hohenzollern Redoubt—Lens—The Lorette Spur   30

CONTENTS

CHAPTER VII

Daily Trips from Doullens: The Allied Spring Offensive of 1917—Vimy Ridge—Lens to Oppy—The Valley of the Scarpe—Arras ... 35

CHAPTER VIII

Daily Trips from Amiens: A Day at Thiepval, Beaumont-Hamel, and the Battlefields of the Ancre—The Somme, Fricourt, Mametz, Montauban, and Longueval—The Woods of the Somme: Bernafay, Mametz, Trones, Delville, and the Bois de Fourneaux 41

CHAPTER IX

The Scenes of the British Retreat in March, 1918: The Most Critical Day of the War—The Thin Khaki Line—German Luck—A Fighting Retreat—Amiens the Best Headquarters—The Long, Straight Road 47

CHAPTER X

From Trenches to War in the Open—The Hundred Days' Battle—Fighting in the Industrial Districts of Belgium—Armistice—Waterloo Revisited—An Interesting Comparison 55

CONCLUSION

The Sentinels 61

ILLUSTRATIONS

THE VICTORY SMILE	*Frontispiece*	
TROOPS RESTING IN A RESERVE TRENCH	*Facing page*	6
A WORKING PARTY ASSEMBLING PRIOR TO A NIGHT'S HARD DIGGING ...	,,	7
1. CAVALRY AND CYCLISTS MOVING THROUGH A RUINED VILLAGE.—2. HOW THE TROOPS ARE FED: RATIONS FOR THE FRONT LINE ...	,,	14
1. DINNER BEING CARRIED TO THE FRONT LINE TRENCHES.—2. THE MUD OF FLANDERS	,,	15
A PARTY OF SAPPERS ON THE MENIN ROAD	,,	22
1. A "HEAVY" GUN READY FOR ACTION.—A LIGHT HOWITZER GUN IN ACTION	,,	23
1. A TRENCH IN HIGH WOOD AFTER A BOMBARDMENT. — 2. A USEFUL BRIDGE CAUSED BY A FALLEN TREE	,,	30
FROM TRENCHES TO THE OPEN	,,	31
HOTEL DE VILLE, ARRAS	,,	38
SCENE IN A FRONT LINE TRENCH ...	,,	39
1. A HUGE SHELL CRATER IN MAMETZ WOOD.—2. REMAINS OF A MACHINE GUN PLATFORM IN A TREE ...	,,	46
A COMMUNICATION TRENCH THROUGH A WOOD	,,	47
1. FORWARD OBSERVATION OFFICER ENGAGED IN "REGISTERING" ON PROMINENT FEATURES OF THE ENEMY'S LINE.—2. A HIGH VELOCITY NAVAL GUN READY TO FIRE	,,	48

ILLUSTRATIONS

TROOPS ADVANCING THROUGH A RUINED TOWN	*Facing page* 49
A TANK IN DIFFICULTIES	,, 52
1. COLOGNE AS SEEN FROM AN AEROPLANE.—2. VICTORY! THE BRITISH OCCUPATION OF COLOGNE.—3. TANKS IN REVIEW ORDER OUTSIDE COLOGNE CATHEDRAL	,, 53

MAPS.

YPRES AND DISTRICT	*Facing page* 18
LILLE AND DISTRICT	,, 26
THE BLACK COUNTRY OF FRANCE	,, 33
THE VALLEY OF THE SCARPE	,, 35
THE SOMME AND THE ANCRE	,, 41

INTRODUCTION

NATURE is hard at work on the battlefields, nursing them back to health and peace. She has it all her own way now. Already many of the scars of war have softened down : soon they will be gone altogether, and the old familiar landmarks will be things of the past. It will be no easy matter to pick up the trench lines and to recognize the various positions held by ourselves and the enemy. It will be harder still to picture those days of mud and strife and dreariness, and to see with the mind's eye life as it used to be on the western front.

It is hoped, however, that this little handbook, in addition to being a guide to places of interest, will also help the tourist to recast some of the stirring scenes of the battlefields, and to realize what war meant to the man in the front line. With this end in view, the author has endeavoured to give a short outline of things that happened on the battle fronts, as well as some hints on how to get there and what to look for.

Needless to say, the book is by no means complete. It deals only with those bits of the line in which the author served and fought. Over four years of war, however, brought him to nearly every important battle from the Yser to the Somme, including the retreat of March, 1918, as well as the final Allied advance to Victory. He has been fortunate, too, in being able to revisit many of his old haunts and examine the picture without fear of a "protest" from the man "across the way."

T. A. L.

February 8th, 1920.

THE WESTERN BATTLEFIELDS

CHAPTER I

PRELIMINARY PLANS — WALKING THE BEST METHOD OF PROGRESS—WHAT TO WEAR—WHAT TO TAKE—WHAT TO AVOID.

Preliminary Plans.

MUCH of the success of a tour to the battlefields will depend on the plans and arrangements made before starting. Even if the tourist intends joining a party accompanied by a travelling guide, he will be well advised to read up beforehand with the aid of a good map the details which interest him most. He will then be independent of the guide, and will find himself able to roam at will over the ground and visit those spots which for various reasons may be sacred to him. It may be the road where working parties and reliefs edged up to the line at night, the scene of some patrol incident in No Man's Land, or the attack on a wood or village. The great thing to aim at is to get to the spot one wants to see, and to lose no time in getting there. Therefore let the tourist work out his tour beforehand; he will find that time and trouble spent over these plans will repay him with compound interest. It will be a good plan, too, if one of the party can go on ahead to make arrangements about accommodation and details of each day's trip.

The Western Battlefields

During the war maps were issued showing the lines of the trenches and the positions of headquarters. Some of these are still in existence, and many officers and men who fought in France and Belgium would probably supply tracings for use with ordinary maps, of which the *carte routiere* of Northern France, published by A. Taride of Paris, is probably as good as any.

Walking the Best Method of Progress.

The best way to tour the battlefields is to walk them. A motor or train is all very well up to a certain point, but there is nothing like walking if one wants to visit the places where things happened and men fought. Walking has the additional advantage of being the most inexpensive method of travel, and the poor man will have the consolation of knowing that by walking he is seeing a great deal more of the detail of the country than the motorist could possibly see. Also, as the majority of the troops employed in the war were infantrymen, he will feel that he is tramping as they were obliged to tramp, minus the burden of a rifle, equipment, and heavy pack—details which are well calculated to minimize the delights of a walking tour.

But he is warned that there is little use undertaking long, daily tramps over the battlefields, unless he is physically fit to stand the strain before he begins, no matter how enthusiastic he may feel. A blistered heel or a swollen leg may add a realistic touch to the pilgrimage, but either may soon spoil the interest of the scene, and be the cause of a rapid return to England before the tour is well started.

Preliminary Plans

What to Wear.

As for clothes, an old golfing suit is the most suitable, with stout boots and leggings : the latter protect the shins against sharp ends of wire, for there is still a certain amount lying about in the undergrowth. A mackintosh coat or cape should always be carried except when there is no doubt about the weather ; it gives little trouble when rolled on the back between the shoulders. Ladies should wear strong boots, thick woollen stockings, and short skirts, with a woollen jumper or jersey, if they wish to really enjoy the tour. The country is so rough that any lighter form of kit would be absurd. Field glasses and a camera complete the outfit, except that I strongly recommend the addition of a small First Aid outfit containing some antiseptic which can be dabbed on cuts and scratches.

I have said nothing about provision for the inner man—tastes differ on that subject ; but personally I always carry sandwiches and something to drink on these journeys, and the tourist will be well advised to provide himself with a light midday meal.

What to Avoid.

Last, but by no means least, old shells and bombs. Some of these souvenirs are still lying about in unexplored places. They have a nasty way of waking up even after long years of repose. If you are not tired of life, leave them well alone. Already, I see, a small party of tourists has had the misfortune to become seriously injured by the explosion of a gas shell inadvertently kicked by one of them when jumping over an old trench. I also know of a lady who, in stooping to pick up what she imagined to be a " souvenir," sustained a great shock in discovering that it was really an old boot, and that inside the boot were human bones. The best and most useful kind of souvenirs are old empty shell cases, which can easily be found. They can be polished up brightly, and make beautiful vases and flower-pots.

CHAPTER II

THE JOURNEY FROM ENGLAND—FOLKESTONE TO BOULOGNE, THE MAIN ARTERY OF COMMUNICATIONS DURING THE WAR—OTHER ROUTES—A DAY IN BOULOGNE—THE PLAN OF THE BOOK.

THE original British Expeditionary Force landed in France on 13th August, 1914, and in writing of the disembarkation of the troops, a famous historian of the Great War says: "All France broke into a smile at the sight of them, and it was at a moment when a smile meant much to France."

The visitor to the Western Battlefields, as he disembarks at Boulogne, Rouen, or Havre, will do well to visualize the scene—the long lines of khaki soldiers streaming down the gangways of transports; the march through beautiful streets crowded with astonished natives almost unable to believe the evidence of their own eyes; the quick beat of the drums heading each column, and the choruses of "Tipperary" or "Here we are, here we are, here we are again" ringing through the ranks. From that moment the *entente cordiale* between France and England became a thing unlike any previous alliance between nations: it became a deep and everlasting friendship, based on common sorrows, common hardship, and common joys. No Frenchman who watched the British Army landing in France in that fateful month can speak

The Western Battlefields

of it without tears in his eyes; no Britisher who belonged to the force which was landing (and, alas! there are but few left to tell the tale) who did not feel himself thrill as he disembarked in the country he had been sent to help in her great need.

Folkestone to Boulogne.

The main artery of our communications during the war was the route by Folkestone and Boulogne. There were several others, of course—the most important being Southampton and Havre, the route by which millions of tons of heavy baggage and stores were transported; and Dover and Calais, the great channel of ammunition and heavy ordnance. But from Folkestone to Boulogne travelled the majority of the troops, and by this famous route the King's messenger, with his precious dispatch case bearing the latest tidings of victory or disaster could be found travelling, guarded closely from too inquisitive eyes.

A great advantage of the Folkestone to Boulogne route, to the civilian traveller, is that he will arrive in Boulogne about seven o'clock in the evening, in plenty of time to find a room in one of its many excellent hotels. During the war Boulogne became practically an English city; that is to say, a very large proportion of its inhabitants were British. There were huge rest camps for troops going on leave and returning from leave, situated near the harbour; hospitals sprang up in every direction, and were perpetually full of wounded soldiers; thousands of officers and clerks were employed upon the duties connected with a huge base.

Official Photograph.]

Between Battles: Troops Resting in a Reserve Trench.

Official Photograph.] **A Working Party Assembling Prior to a Night's Hard Digging.**
When not actually holding Front-Line Positions the Infantry were usually employed as above.
Note Gum Boots Thigh, and Waterproof Sheets converted into Capes.

The Journey from England

Boulogne, a Characteristically French Town.

Nevertheless, to the visitor arriving at Boulogne to-day, there will appear to be surprising little evidence of the British occupation; it is a characteristically French town, and the inhabitants are much prouder of the fact that Napoleon's grand army massed there in 1814 than they are (at present, anyhow) of the British occupation of 1914. Not that I mean to infer that they have not been hospitality and kindness personified; in fact, if you walk into the museum there, you will find cut in a marble tablet on the side of the staircase the following inscription: "France and England have more good sense than all the world." Who wrote it, or why, I failed to discover, but it struck me that this touching little text inscribed long before the war was almost a prophecy, and that it was very fittingly displayed in the city where the two nations were to meet in a common cause.

Where to Sleep.

However, to return to our traveller and his anxiety upon arrival as to where to lay his weary head, I can confidently recommend three hotels—the Folkestone, comfortable but expensive, and therefore much frequented during the war by General and Staff Officers; the Maurice, quiet and genteel, and rather less expensive; and the Louvre, a large and rambling building, where a large number of people can find accommodation at fairly reasonable rates. It might be well to explain that what I mean by " reasonable " is a comfortable bedroom at ten francs a night, and meals from about five francs each, according to

The Western Battlefields

standard, which I think will be found to be about as cheap as can be discovered in France.

Base Hospital Cemeteries.

Also I must not forget that there are many thousands of people whose pilgrimage will end at Boulogne itself, for there is a huge British cemetery on the road to Wimereux consecrated to those who died in the base hospitals there. This cemetery, like those of the other big hospital bases at Etaples, Rouen, Havre, and Calais, gives the impression of a forest of white crosses, but every cross has a name carefully inscribed upon it, and there is a register in possession of the official in charge, by which particular graves can be quickly located.

But our visitor contemplating a battlefield tour either from the point of view of interest or sentiment is merely at the jumping-off place of his tour when he reaches Boulogne. From there he must press on by train or motor to Poperinghe, St. Pol, Lille, Doullens, or Amiens, and fortunately for him, if he be a man of moderate means, train fares in France and Belgium are inexpensive, and he can reach any of these cities for a few francs.

The Plan of the Book.

The plan upon which this little book is built is a simple one, and can be easily followed by those who are unfamiliar with travel in France and Belgium. The towns of Poperinghe, Lille, St. Pol, Doullens, and Amiens have been chosen, and described as "key" towns to the many battlefields in their vicinity. These five centres are all within easy reach by rail of the great seaports, Havre, Rouen, Boulogne, and Calais, which acted

The Journey from England

as the principal bases to the B.E.F. during the war, so that any route from England which the tourist may choose will be suitable.

The "key" towns, it is suggested, will become excellent centres for rest and accommodation; the tourist may find himself occupying the same quarters in many cases that the troops occupied when resting behind the lines; he will dine in the same little restaurants, or even private houses, at small cost, in exactly the same manner that officers and men used to do; he will smoke his cigarette or cigar in the evenings with the same friendly inhabitants who so cheerfully endured the occupation of a huge army in their midst for five weary years, and hear from them much that will interest and amaze him. The "atmosphere" of the great campaign will soon be acquired, and the imagination stimulated.

For touring battlefields is a different thing altogether to touring for the purpose of sight-seeing; in fact, I can safely say that the mere sight-seer will probably be disappointed with the devastated zones of France and Belgium. But combined with "atmosphere" and imagination they will draw the tourist like magnets, and he will probably return to them again and again.

The Daily Trips.

From each of the "key" towns daily trips have been marked out. They are not laid down in any hard-and-fast manner, for the tourist may prefer to ramble about in his own way, or he may have his own definite objectives to reach which are not described. But these daily trips are given with a view to help those who wish to visit the scenes of great battles, and little incidents in connection

with each have been described, and may convey to the reader still further " atmosphere."

For obvious reasons no daily trips have been mapped out to the areas in which the great French and American battles took place, the most obvious being that each of these would require a book unto themselves, and, secondly, because the writer is a British officer, and served during the war only in the areas occupied by British troops. But in many of the sectors covered by the daily trips described, French, British, and American armies were working together in the common cause.

CHAPTER III

THE "KEY" TOWNS: POPERINGHE, THE KEY TO FLANDERS—LILLE, THE KEY TO PLOEGSTEERT WOOD, ARMENTIERES, AND GIVENCHY—ST. POL, THE KEY TO LA BASSEE, LENS, LOOS, AND VIMY—DOULLENS, THE KEY TO ARRAS—AMIENS, THE KEY TO THE SOMME.

Poperinghe, the Key to Flanders.

IT cannot, even by a stretch of the imagination, be said that the city of Poperinghe—or "Pop," as it was more familiarly known to the Army—is a beautiful one. In fact, there are few cities that I know, of less attraction to the eye, although it contains many fine buildings. Yet the truth remains that during the weary years of trench warfare in the Ypres Salient, Poperinghe stood for everything that meant civilization to the British Army. The road from Poperinghe to Ypres was known to every soldier: to march eastwards on this road meant work, trenches, mud—everything unpleasant; to march westwards meant rest, a "comfy" dinner in the town, and possibly an evening at the club. Needless to say, the latter comforts were only enjoyed occasionally and at long intervals, so "Pop" was a city beloved by the Army; its fame will live, together with that of Bailleul, Bethune, Doullens, and Amiens, as a hospitable and pleasant city. To turn out in one's best kit and walk again upon a pavement; to gaze into clean shop windows; to drop into

The Western Battlefields

"Skindle's" for tea or for a drink, served by a bevy of bright, fresh-looking merry girls, with whom every subaltern in the Army was in love; to dine at the club—these were pleasures which could only be properly appreciated after a month's existence in the trenches. We never knew how much they meant to us until we lost them. "Pop" became a skeleton of its former self, from which the inhabitants were forced to flee; Bailleul is now a heap of ruins; Bethune is unrecognizable; Doullens and Amiens are sadly changed. But they were all fair cities in their day, and will live for ever in the affections of the survivors of the British Expeditionary Force.

To Poperinghe, therefore, the visitor is advised to journey if his object be to make a study of the Ypres Salient. No fears need be entertained about comfortable accommodation, for although the city was shelled frequently and heavily, it yet preserved its outline in a truly miraculous fashion. The inhabitants have returned, damaged houses have been repaired, new hotels, restaurants and boarding-houses have sprung up in every direction. The road to Ypres from Poperinghe covers a short distance of but six miles.

Lille, the Key to Ploegsteert Wood, Armentieres, and Givenchy.

There is no more interesting battle line than that which in 1915 stretched from the southern flank of the Ypres Salient to the coalfields of Loos. It includes the famous Ploegsteert Wood; the scenes of the fight for the Aubers Ridge; the ruins of Armentieres; and the craters of Givenchy. It is crammed with memories of exciting raids, hurricane bombardments, and fierce hand-to-hand fighting.

The "Key" Towns

This part of the line may be toured in one day if the tourist crosses over to what was then enemy country, and makes his headquarters where the Germans had theirs—in Lille. The town is an interesting one, and is well supplied with good hotels. In spite of the fact that it remained in German hands during the greater part of the war, it suffered less in the way of bombardment than any other town in the vicinity of the front line. During the great Allied advance of the autumn of 1918, Lille became the headquarters of the Fifth Army, and for months after the Armistice was signed it became the centre of the social life of that part of the British Army which did not immediately advance into Germany. From Lille many thousands of demobilized officers and soldiers set out upon their final journey to home and civil employment, as one of the main dispersal camps was quartered there for many months.

There was an officers' club in Lille, next door to the beautiful Opera House, run by the Expeditionary Force Canteen. In October, 1918, it was a German officers' club, and there was only an interval of a fortnight between the changes of management. It was originally a first-class hotel, but the Germans converted it into a sort of palace for their officers resting after labours in the trenches. In the same way they sent their very best operatic companies from Berlin to the Opera House next door, for the entertainment of troops billeted in Lille.

But when the British occupied Lille they were not to be outdone in this manner. British operatic companies could not, of course, be obtained; but Mr. Leslie Henson, the famous comedian, who was then serving with the Fifth Army, organized a

The Western Battlefields

pantomime entirely composed of soldiers, to which entertainment the civilian population were admitted. The theatre was packed twice daily, and the audience spent two delightful hours rocking with laughter at the gifted band of "amateurs." This, together with the universal courtesy and kindness of the British, did much to help the inhabitants of Lille to throw off the deadly yoke under which they had suffered for so many years.

The visitor will have a kindly reception should he decide to break his journey at Lille.

St. Pol, the Key to La Bassee, Lens, Loos, and Vimy.

Many famous battlefields may be visited daily if the town of St. Pol is chosen as a temporary headquarters by the visitor. The distance from the "front" is greater than is the case with Poperinghe and Lille, but communication by rail to Arras has been re-established, and from Arras places such as Vimy, Souchez, Lens, and Loos may be reached within the day.

The line from St. Pol to Bethune is also in full swing, and from here our visitor may study the battlefields of Festubert, Givenchy, La Bassee and the Hohenzollern Redoubt.

There is not much of actual war interest to be seen in the town of St. Pol itself, as it came through the campaign almost unscathed, but there is plenty of accommodation to be found, and a couple of excellent restaurants, so that as a centre for this part of the line it is to be recommended, though Lille will be found the more convenient from the point of view of distance and accommodation to the northern part of this line.

Official Photographs.]

1. Cavalry and Cyclists moving through a Ruined Village.
2. How the Troops are Fed—Rations for the Front Line.

Official] 1. **Dinner Being Carried to the Front Line Trenches.** [Photograph.
It has been Cooked in Field Kitchens behind.
2. **The Mud of Flanders.**
This picture is typical of the prevailing conditions during the Winter months.

The "Key" Towns

Doullens, the Key to the Ancre.

In a similar manner the town of Doullens may be chosen as a centre from which daily trips to the battlefields can be made. During the war the town was an important railway junction for the lateral communications of the Allied armies, and it was there that Marshal Foch and Field Marshal Lord Haig met to discuss the critical situation of the great German advance in March, 1918, and where the supreme command of the Allied armies was formally handed over to the former. An association such as this will in itself be the cause of historical fame to Doullens, although it was famous enough to every soldier by reason of the fact that every train carrying troops to the Ancre battlefields passed through it.

From Doullens places such as Gommecourt, Achiet-le-Grand, Hebuterne, Mailly-Mailly, Pusieux, and Serre may be reached within the day; while at Beauval, but three miles away, can be seen the great flat fields which acted as one of the largest aeroplane centres of the war.

Doullens boasts of several comfortable hotels and cafés, while all the surrounding villages are noted for the hospitality of their inhabitants to British troops.

Amiens, the Key to the Somme.

Once upon a time, when engaged in censoring some letters—that miserable task which was hated as much by the officers who had to perform it as it was by the men whose letters required to be censored—I read the following:—"We are now billeted at a place which has a name like Amiens Street Station in Dublin." That was in

the early summer of 1916, when a goodly portion of the British Army was concentrated in the neighbourhood of Amiens, prior to the great attack of July 1st. And a very delightful country it was: beautiful woods, full of shady trees; cool rivers, pleasant to bathe in; happy, smiling villages, inhabited by simple and hospitable villagers; and, last, but not least, the lovely city of Amiens, with its open-air cafés and tempting shop-windows, brim full of life and interest. It is said during the great retreat of March, 1918, when Amiens was being heavily shelled by the Germans, and everything pointed to the city being overrun by the enemy, that the old burgomaster rent his clothes and cursed the British for their infidelity. But it is pleasing to know that the same dear old gentleman, whom many of us had the pleasure to meet personally, welcomed General Birdwood and a small contingent of Australians as the "saviours of my beloved city." For Amiens was not quite captured in that ferocious rush of March and April, 1918, but how nearly it escaped will be the chief object of interest to visitors for the next half-century.

On arrival at Amiens the visitor may well stand for a few moments and gaze at the glass roof of the station. It is mended now, but there are still traces of the havoc wrought by the huge German shells which pounded through it, with the object of spoiling the great railway junction, and thereby completely separating the French and British Armies.

Then, as the traveller walks out into the street, he will be able to realize how the whole neighbourhood of the station suffered too. Hotels, houses, and shops are still in various stages of repair. So

The "Key" Towns

much is this so that it is useless to recommend the name of any particular hotel in Amiens which was good before the city was bombarded; nearly all of them were hit, and some may never be rebuilt. But at the same time I can assure the visitor that he will have no difficulty in obtaining cheap and comfortable accommodation in the city, because the inhabitants are of a thrifty and industrious disposition, and are quickly completing arrangements to welcome the large number of tourists who will flock to their city for sight-seeing. One place I know did escape—the Restaurant Godbert, where most excellent meals can be obtained. This was the rendezvous of the British officer, young and old, from Field Marshal to subaltern, during the war. The dining-room is a huge place full of small tables, and the waitresses—cheery girls who speak English perfectly by this time—will tell of the escapades of the " mad " officers who were wont to enjoy their fleeting moments of leave there. And that those escapades were as harmless as they were amusing and jolly, the staff of the " Godbert " are the first to admit.

Five miles to the east of Amiens lies the village of Villers-Bretonneux, which may fittingly be described as the high-tide mark of the whole campaign in the West. There is a stone placed upon the road to mark the spot where the German advanced guard of the last great offensive stopped. It is at the foot of a small hill, which, if the visitor will take the trouble to climb, will afford to him a view of the coveted Amiens, and, a few miles to the westward, the sea !

But no Boche was ever destined to gloat over that fair vision.

CHAPTER IV

DAILY TRIPS FROM POPERINGHE: A VISIT TO THE YSER CANAL—PILKEM AND ST. JULIEN—A DAY AT HOOGE AND GHELUVELT—KEMMEL, WYTSCHAETE, AND THE MESSINES RIDGE — HOW TO REACH PASSCHENDAELE.

A Visit to the Yser Canal.

NEARLY everybody who fought in the Ypres Salient halted for a period at the Yser Canal. During four long years that short strip of canalized water between Boesinghe and Ypres was at once the terror and the refuge of hundreds of thousands of British soldiers moving to and from the trenches to the east of it—the terror, because of the bridges which had to be crossed, the range of which were known to an inch by every German gunner; the refuge, because of the hospitable banks which millions of high explosives failed to destroy, and which our engineers and tunnellers successfully converted into safe and comfortable habitations. From an international point of view, also, there are few more interesting spots on the Western Front; the Belgian, French, and British Armies all had their share in the fierce fighting which occurred in the neighbourhood of Boesinghe. In fact, it could be stated with truth that the Yser Canal was the centre of a continuous battle which lasted for over four years, and in which nearly every division in the British Army was at some period employed.

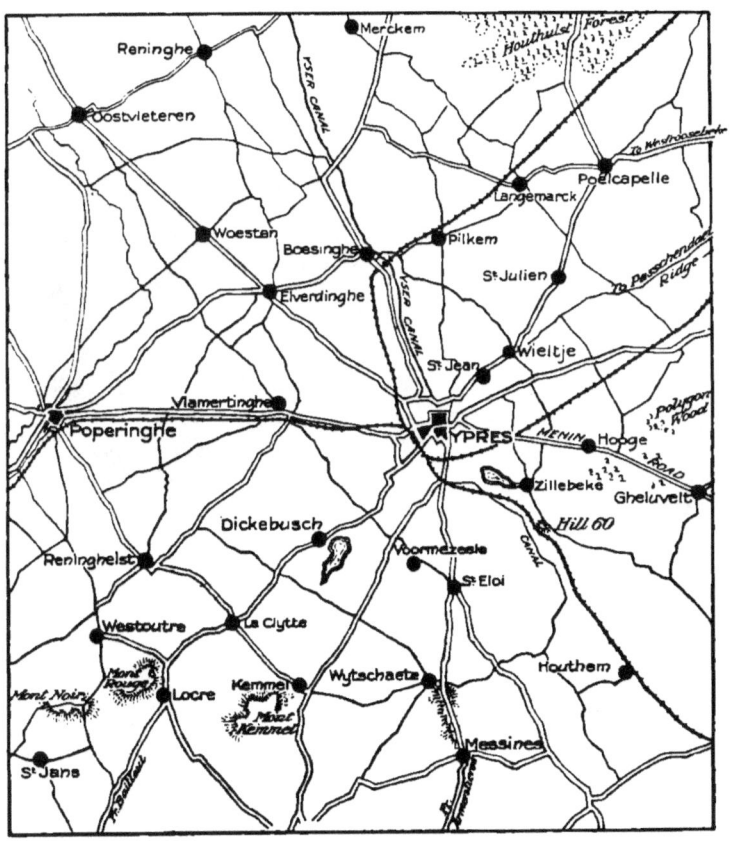

YPRES AND DISTRICT

Daily Trips from Poperinghe

To reach the Yser Canal from Poperinghe is a simple matter. It is but seven miles either to Elverdinghe or Vlamertinghe, the two famous villages which formed the base of perhaps the most unpleasant triangle of roads that troops have ever had to traverse. There is much of interest by the way: miles of hastily constructed trenches, cunningly devised to maintain the Allied footing in Belgium at all costs, should the front-line positions be penetrated; ancient châteaux, heavily sandbagged, and camouflaged as observation posts, whose cellars sheltered many important commands; emplacements for guns of all calibres, whose barrage lines were literally as the pencil of a compass describing the half of a circle. Another mile by either road, and the canal is reached. A glance will show the tactical importance of the place to the least observant, and the reason why the Germans made such frantic efforts to capture it. It forms the diameter of the Ypres Salient, and consequently was used as the supporting position to shelter nearly all reserve troops employed by the Allies in defending that city. With the Yser Canal in their possession, the Germans might easily have occupied the whole of Belgium.

Pilkem and St. Julien.

Crossing the Yser Canal by the Pont de Boesinghe, a short walk will bring the visitor to what remains of the village of Pilkem. Fighting of the most continued and ferocious character took place over the small ridge upon which this village is situated. Upon every side lies a scene of desolation which would be difficult to describe. It is doubtful whether anyone could point out now where the actual front-line trenches were situated,

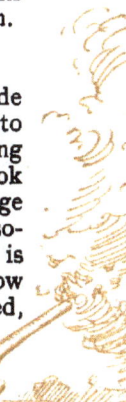

so uniformly shell-beaten has the whole sector become. But the progress of the fighting, and a large number of the units engaged, can be traced by a study of the wayside cemeteries. The history of the Allied efforts here is perhaps better written than it could possibly be written by an historian in the tiny forests of white crosses indicating the last resting places of the warriors who fought and eventually conquered.

The same applies to St. Julien. To reach this famous village, the Yser Canal should be crossed by a wooden bridge half a mile north of Ypres, known as No. 5 Bridge, on the Brielen Road. A walk of some five miles will reveal the remains of the villages of St. Jean and Wieltje, the latter famous for a tunnel capable of sheltering a whole battalion of infantry in case of need. Between Wieltje and St. Julien the old front line of the salient will be seen, if enough remains of it to be recognized as such.

Many unsuccessful attempts were made by the British to capture St. Julien, until the Third Battle of Ypres, in 1917, when they gained possession of it for a time.

A Day at Hooge and Gheluvelt.

The Menin Road—what visions of effort, struggle and bloodshed the very words conjure up! Beginning with the immortal struggle of the 7th Division in 1914, the Menin Road from Ypres to Gheluvelt was the scene of continual fighting during the whole course of the war. Before leaving Ypres by the Menin Gate, the visitor should study the famous ramparts, built in ancient times as a defence of the city against marauding bands, and so stoutly constructed that they were

Daily Trips from Poperinghe

able to withstand the very heaviest shell the Germans could construct in the Great War. Ramparts, indeed, they were, and perhaps better deserving of the name than the most modern of concrete constructions of later years.

The Menin Road is a long, straight *pavé* road, wide enough in most parts for three motor lorries to travel abreast, and by one of those curious freaks of fortune so strongly built that, except where trenches were cut across it, it withstood the withering rain of shells to which it was subjected for four years without showing very great signs of wear. From Ypres to Gheluvelt is a distance of four miles, and if the traveller desires to make the most of it he is advised to walk. To the south he will see Zillebeke and Zillebeke Lake, while to the north-east can be seen the long, straight line of the Passchendaele Ridge, flanked by the misty outline of the famous Houthulst Forest.

On the road itself Hooge is quickly reached, and a view obtained of the smashed and withered stumps which are now all that is left to represent Inverness Copse and Polygon Wood. This is the scene of the tank disaster of August, 1917, and the remains of many of these heroic monsters, which, with their crews, perished in the unconquerable mud of that unhappy battle, can still be seen scattered as far as Westhoek. Gheluvelt itself exists but in name, but a name perhaps more closely connected with the defence of the Channel Ports than any other, for it was here that the 2nd Battalion of the Worcester Regiment barred the path to what would certainly have become a triumphant German march to Calais.

From that date—29th October, 1914—there was a continuous swaying battle between Hooge and

Gheluvelt until 28th September, 1918. Truly the Germans did not love the Menin Road; it was too intimately connected with their soul-destroying proverb, "See Ypres and die." And it can be said that more Germans died on the Menin Road and its vicinity than on any other part of the Western Front.

Kemmel, Wytschaete, and the Messines Ridge.

To the south of Ypres are situated very many places intimately connected with the long-drawn-out trench warfare of 1915, 1916, and part of 1917. Every road, every stream, every village was known at some time during these periods to the divisions whose task it was to defend them. Nothing could have been more unsuitable from a tactical point of view than the positions which were held by the British in this neighbourhood. The front line ran through St. Eloi and southwards to the western slopes of the Messines Ridge, and without exception any advantage of rising ground was in the possession of the Germans. What this meant can only be realized by a study of the ground in the winter time. The soil is of clay and difficult to drain, and in some cases our trenches actually ran through great swamps, which without tremendous exertion in pumping would have become a series of miniature canals. This was the country in which the troops could only exist in the winter time by using gum boots which reached to the thigh, where pumps were working continuously in every fire bay, where shelter could only be obtained by the use of ready-made steel plates, known as "elephants," made in England and shipped complete with bolts and screws to a standard design. Yet before any of these things

Official Photograph.]

A Party of Sappers on the Menin Road.
The water to the right is not a Canal, it is merely a series of Shell Holes caused by some of the "Heavies" which burst continuously in this neighbourhood for four-and-a-half years.

Official Photographs. A "Heavy" Gun Ready for Action. A Light Howitzer Gun in Action.
Note Ammunition Limbers returning from *Field Gun Batteries in Front.*

Daily Trips from Poperinghe

arrived the line was held, and stoutly held, without them, but only by enormous sacrifice of officers and men to the dreadful plague of frost-bite and "trench feet."

The road from Ypres through Voormezeele to La Clytte, a distance of about four miles, should be studied. It ran parallel to the old front line, and such was the observation which the heights of Wytschaete and the Messines Ridge afforded to the enemy that the movement of a rabbit upon it could be seen in daylight. Yet at night the traffic of relieving units and ration parties upon it was unceasing, though at intervals it would be swept with shell fire.

But one great advantage which the British enjoyed in this neighbourhood was the possession of Mont Kemmel. This little hill was the "eye" of the Second Army for long years until the Germans captured it in the dark days of April, 1918. Spacious dug-outs and tunnels were mined in it, and from its many observation posts the fire of most of the heavy batteries defending the salient was directed. From the "O.Ps." in Mont Kemmel most of the trenches as far north as Pilkem could be seen on a clear day, and when the atmosphere was particularly favourable it was possible even to view the sea in the direction of Ostend and Nieuport.

The visitor should seize the opportunity of spending a few hours on the top of Kemmel with map and guide; he will be rewarded for his climb.

He will also realize how adversely the capture of Mont Kemmel by the Germans in 1918 affected the fortunes of the Allies. The line was forced back then as far as Locre, and the city of Bailleul, previously a haven of refuge for troops in rest,

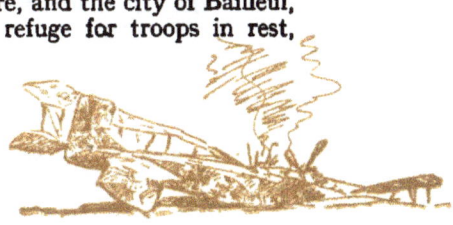

was captured and shelled to ruins. Fortunately, however, the line of hills, Mont Rouge, Mont Noir, and Mont des Cats remained in our possession, and to a certain extent still supplied the observation which was lost with Kemmel.

The actual capture of Kemmel from the French in 1918 was one of the bloodiest engagements of the war. By a prolonged bombardment of gas shells unequalled in intensity, a whole division was put out of action and the hill was taken. But the Germans were not to enjoy its advantages for long, for in August, 1918, they were driven from its slopes by a combined attack of British and American troops.

No description of this neighbourhood would be complete without reference to the famous Messines Ridge. The village of Messines lies to the east of Mont Kemmel, a distance of five miles. Perhaps the most brilliant operation of the whole war in its completeness and the careful detail in which it was carried out was the capture of this ridge from Wytschaete to Messines in June, 1917, by General Plumer's Army. It has been called the Battle of the Mines, by reason of the fact that nineteen enormous mines, some of which had taken years to construct, were blown in the enemy's lines as a preliminary to the assault. The craters of these can still be seen, the most interesting being those at Hill 60 and St. Eloi.

How to reach Passchendaele.

Another daily trip from Poperinghe which should not be missed is a visit to the Passchendaele Ridge. I have purposely left this to the end of this chapter because the distance entailed being greater, transport of some kind will be required.

Daily Trips from Poperinghe

The distance from Ypres to Zonnebeke is seven miles, and from there the road runs due north along the whole of the Passchendaele Ridge to Westroosebeke. The village of Passchendaele itself was captured by the Canadians in October, 1917, after a mighty struggle, the traces of which remain on every side to this day. This was the culminating effort of the great fighting in Flanders in 1917. But here again the British triumph was but momentary, and after holding the main part of the ridge for the winter of 1917-18 our troops were compelled to withdraw before the great enemy offensive of April, 1918. Eventually the ridge was recaptured by the Belgians in October, 1918, in the outflanking operation under the King of the Belgians. Some idea of the impassable nature of the ground can be obtained when it is realized that during this great battle the roads could not be used, and the Belgians on the Passchendaele Ridge had to be fed by aeroplanes which dropped their rations on selected dumps, and so enabled them to maintain their positions.

CHAPTER V

DAILY TRIPS FROM LILLE : ARMENTIERES—PLOEG-
STEERT WOOD—NEUVE CHAPELLE—FESTU-
BERT AND GIVENCHY.

Armentieres.

THE best way to tour the battlefields from Lille is to take the road to Armentieres, a distance of about eight miles. Lille was originally a fortified city, and the visitor, if he chooses this road, will pass through the old ramparts—quite an interesting study in themselves. The country between Lille and Armentieres is very flat, and there is little of interest by the way for the first three or four miles, but traces will soon be found of the elaborate defences which the Germans prepared in defence of the town. There were literally forests of barbed wire erected across this road, while line after line of elaborate trench systems remain to illustrate the importance which the Germans attached to its defence. Gradually, as the old trench line is reached, the whole country for miles becomes a vista of shell-beaten territory. Most of the shell-holes are now overgrown and full of stagnant water, but traces of the old front line and support systems can still be followed.

Armentieres, as it now exists, is a wreck of what was once a prosperous little manufacturing town. For years it existed within a mile or so of the front line, almost untouched, and many of the inhabitants continued in their daily avocations ; but

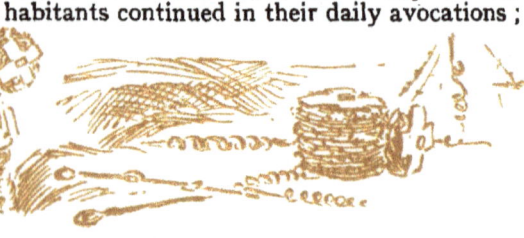

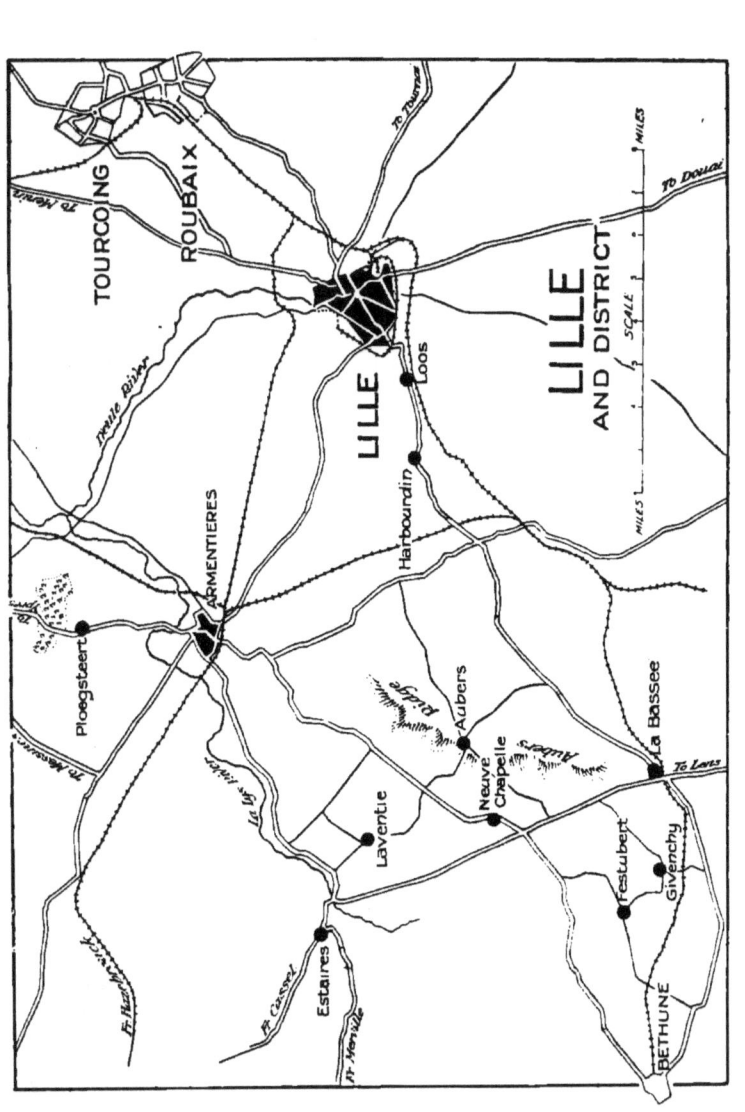

Daily Trips from Lille

in the spring of 1918 it received the full force of the concentrated fury which was thrown into the German effort to break through to the Channel ports in conjunction with the attack upon Amiens in the south. Armentieres was destroyed by this attack, and the weight of heavy ordnance which was thrown into it was terrific. But for many years it was well known to the British Army, particularly to the 6th Division, which spent many comfortable months in its vicinity.

Ploegsteert Wood.

To visit the famous " Plug Street " Wood, the visitor should work northwards from Armentieres, a journey of three miles, to the village of Ploegsteert. Nothing particularly remarkable now remains of the wood which takes its name from the village, nevertheless it is worth a visit, as it is one of the really historical spots of the Western Front. It was what became known as a " cushy " place for many years—that is, a sector of the British front which was neither particularly uncomfortable nor particularly dangerous. The place was seldom shelled by the Germans, although it contained elaborate systems of trenches. In the winter time drainage was good and dug-outs usually habitable ; in the summer the trees became thick with foliage, and life was exceedingly pleasant as judged by front-line life in other sectors. Yet " Plug Street " Wood was a sinister place, and the proportion of officers and men who lost their lives there by the sniper's bullet a very high one. The peaceable aspect of nature often led men to expose themselves unnecessarily, and sure retribution was certain to follow, as the German marksmen in this neighbourhood were masters of their trade—

a fact to which the many little cemeteries scattered about the Wood bear witness.

Neuve Chapelle.

Another trip from Lille which can be accomplished in a day is the one to Neuve Chapelle and the Aubers Ridge. Returning to Armentieres, the visitor should take the road to the south passing through Laventie, and finally cutting the old British lines near Neuve Chapelle, the scene of the battle in which the Indian Corps and the 4th British Corps took part in March, 1915. This battle was the first offensive on a big scale that the British undertook in the war, and if it had been successful, and the Aubers Ridge—the objective of the attack—had been captured, the road to Lille would have been opened up, and possibly the Manchester of France would have fallen to our arms. But it is well known that this did not happen, although in parts the offensive was a successful one. German barbed wire was the main cause of its general failure, and many thousands of lives were lost in the vain attempt to overcome that obstacle. Still, the Battle of Neuve Chapelle in 1915 may be said to have accomplished much in that it gave the Germans a considerable fright—it is now known that during this battle feverish activity was displayed in Lille in the loading of baggage and preparations for evacuation—and by reason of the fact that it demonstrated many points in relation to modern offensive action, which were usefully practised in later attacks. Also the moral effect of even a partial victory at that time was considerable, the German losses being estimated at 18,000.

Daily Trips from Lille

Festubert and Givenchy.

From three to four miles south-west of Neuve Chapelle lie the remains of the villages of Festubert and Givenchy, names which will ever recall fighting of a continuous nature from beginning to end of the campaign. In this region the Indians attacked, together with the Meerut and Lahore Divisions of British troops, in December, 1914— an attack which was unsuccessful, and quickly followed by a German counter-attack, which caused many casualties. This battle was of a very desperate nature, and lasted over the Christmas of that year, until the village of Givenchy was retaken by a very gallant attack of the 1st Manchester Regiment, which succeeded in re-establishing most of the ground which had been lost in the German counter-attacks. Nearly all the British officers of the Indian Corps were killed and wounded in this engagement, a fact that is often forgotten by critics of the Indian troops in France.

Givenchy again became the scene of a terrific battle in the spring of 1918, when the Portugese Army which was holding the trenches in this neighbourhood were heavily attacked, and the line would have been broken had it not been for the very gallant defence of the 51st Scottish Division, which rushed up to support them, and succeeded brilliantly in defending the sector.

A glance at the map will suffice to show the strategical importance of Festubert and Givenchy from the Allied point of view.

CHAPTER VI

Daily Trips from St. Pol: Loos—The Hohenzollern Redoubt — Lens — The Lorette Spur.

Loos.

In order to make an exhaustive study of the battlefield of Loos, the visitor is advised to make his headquarters at St. Pol rather than at Lille, because, as he will daily approach the scene of the great effort of September 25th, 1915, from the west, he will be thus enabled to obtain a clearer vision of the difficulties of the operation. From St. Pol to Bethune is but a short train journey, and the distance from the latter town to the scene of action but six miles by road. The tourist will now find himself in the Black Country of France, with its slag heaps and iron pit towers, and when he mounts the rise at Hulluch, the old Tower Bridge—a mass of twisted machinery on the top of the slag heap—will come into view, standing up on the Loos crassier, and watching Hill 70. From the Tower Bridge there is a fine view of the whole battlefield of Loos, and the old trenches on the hillside and in the valley. On the right can be seen the double crassier—two fingers of slag pointing towards the east. At one time this was a paradise for the snipers of both sides, for both the Germans and ourselves held bits of it at the same time. In front Hill 70 hides the view, while below is the little village of Loos itself, and away on the left Hulluch Wood and the road to Lille. There

Official Photographs.
1. A Trench in High Wood after a Bombardment.   2. A Useful Bridge caused by a Fallen Tree.

Official Photograph.

From Trenches to the Open.
A Platoon advancing from the last German Reserve Trench into Open Country.

Daily Trips from St. Pol

will be no difficulty in picking out the various places of interest from the Tower Bridge. The pit heads and the villages in the vicinity will help the tourist in setting his map, and in this country there are many landmarks to show the various stages of the great battle.

Of the Battle of Loos itself, little can be said in a small book of this nature by way of description. The main assault took place between the La Bassée Canal in the north to the village of Grenay in the south, a distance of about seven miles, and in it were engaged six British divisions—the largest force up to that time which had been employed by the British in a single offensive operation.

The Hohenzollern Redoubt.

To visit the ground in which the Hohenzollern Redoubt and Fosse 8 are located, the visitor will require to spend another day, unless he be fortunate enough to be possessed of a motor-car. These two places, famous by their continual repetition in the official communiqués of 1915 as the scene of perpetual fighting, are worth a visit if only for the study of the wonderfully constructed German trenches, many traces of which still remain.

It was in the Hohenzollern Redoubt and Fosse 8 —a long slag heap which changed hands many times in the autumn of 1915—that the art of bombing reached its perfection. The place was a maze of trenches running in every direction, and every inch of ground gained by an attack of British bombers had the effect of calling out an immediate counter-attack by German bombers, the latter being very much more plentifully supplied with the necessary bombs for such warfare. Rifles and machine guns were almost useless, as all that could be seen of the enemy was their helmets, as they worked along from traverse to traverse. Such was the nature which modern warfare assumed in this neighbourhood : soldiers had abandoned their rifles as useless ; bayonets became toasting forks ; an enemy in the open, moving above trenches, was unknown. The Redoubt changed hands from British to German about once a week, and no sooner was it in the possession of one than preparations were began by the other to retake it. And always by means of bombing attacks. The visitor will find much food for reflection as he gazes upon this scene.

Lens.

Another interesting day can be spent at Lens, which can now be reached by rail direct from Bethune. The trench line in front of Loos remained in a stationary position until about the middle of 1917. Heavy fighting took place both north and south of the town, but it was not until the Canadian Corps and elements of the 1st British Corps attacked and captured the village of Avion, to the immediate south of Lens, that the Germans seemed to realize how greatly it was threatened. Some idea of the nature of this fighting can be imagined when it is realized that, in the outskirts of Lens, Canadians and Germans in many cases actually occupied different rooms in the same houses, and were accustomed to attack each other by knocking down the intervening walls.

Unquestionably the Canadian Corps would have gained complete possession of Lens at this time, but active operations ceased in the neighbourhood owing to the heavy fighting which was taking place

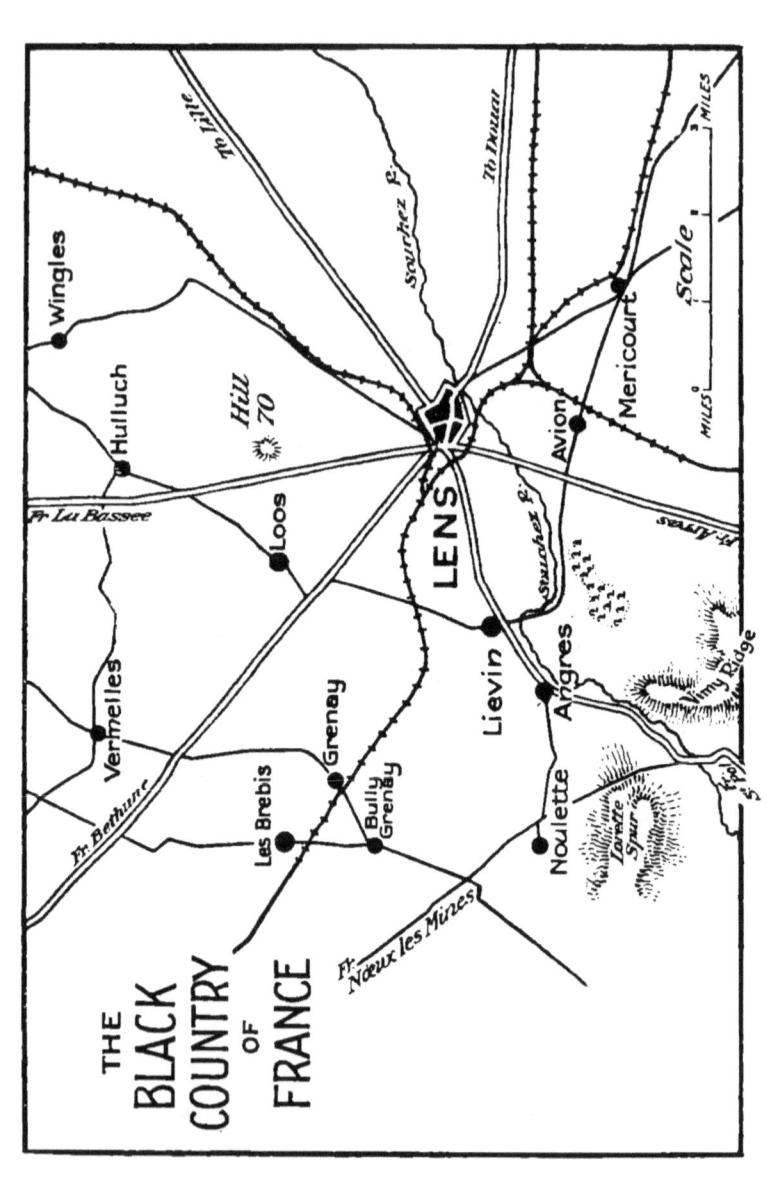

Daily Trips from St. Pol

in the Ypres sector, and the Canadians were transferred to Flanders for the great offensive which captured the Passchendaele Ridge.

From Lens the return journey to St. Pol can be accomplished quickly; but if the tourist wishes to visit the battlefields farther south, he would be well advised to make arrangements for a night's lodging at either Les Brebis or Bully-Grenay, whence he can continue his journey to the scenes of the fighting at Vimy and Arras. Les Brebis and Grenay are mining villages within easy reach of Loos, and they would make handy and comfortable stopping places for those who wish to edge their way gradually southwards. They were at one time rest billets for those troops who held the trench line in front of Loos, and are within easy reach of other towns behind the line, such as Bethune, Noeux-les-Mines, and Bruay.

The Lorette Spur.

From the little mining village of Bully-Grenay, the battlefield of Vimy Ridge may be visited, and Doullens can be taken as the next stopping place. In this way the tourist can work down by easy stages to Amiens, whence daily trips can be made to the battlefields of the Somme, and to the scenes of the fighting of the British retreat in the early days of 1918.

There are many interesting spots on the way. The Bethune—Arras road, running through the little village of Noulette, skirts the Lorette Spur near the Vimy Ridge. This spur in 1915 saw some of the fiercest fighting in which the gallant French Army took part. On the heights of Lorette, near the little shrine bearing that name, our Allies stood against an overwhelming attack, and remained firm against a terrific artillery barrage until the time came for that great counter-attack which sent the enemy back on their line in front of Lens. The battle for the Lorette Spur was a small Verdun; it showed the enemy that the French could convert a defence into a dangerous attack with that speed, dash, and precision which upset more than one of the plans of the German Staff.

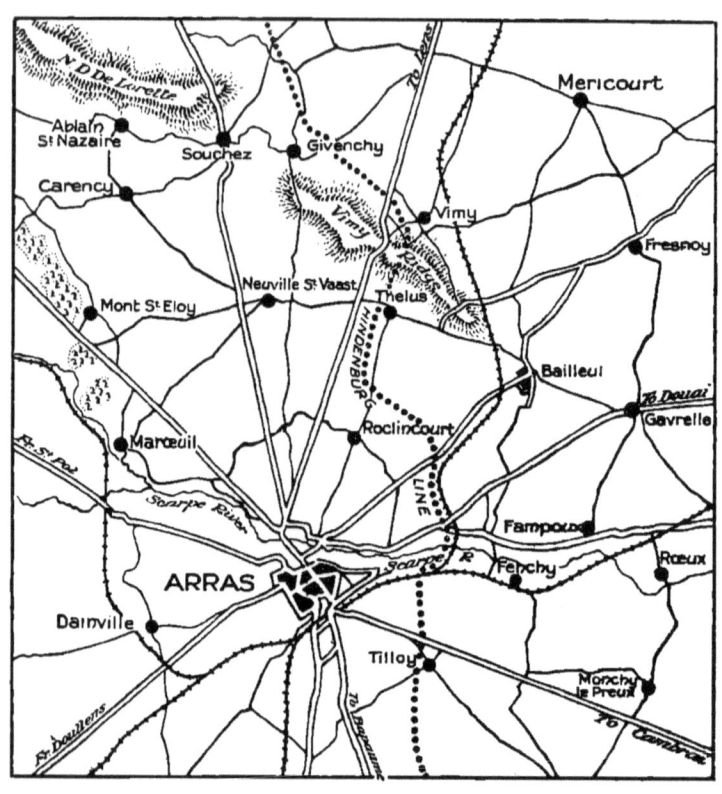

THE VALLEY OF THE SCARPE

CHAPTER VII

Daily Trips from Doullens: The Allied Spring Offensive of 1917—Vimy Ridge—Lens to Oppy—The Valley of the Scarpe—Arras.

The Allied Spring Offensive of 1917.

In the last chapter the tourist was advised to change his headquarters to an intermediate point, and Bully-Grenay was mentioned as a suitable half-way house.

When the time came for the spring offensive of 1917, the British opened the ball with an attack along the Arras front. This attack extended from Vimy Ridge in the north to the village of Croisilles, south-east of Arras, in the south, a distance of about fourteen miles.

In the first place this attack was intended to be in the nature of a feint, to draw the enemy's attention away from other points against which operations on a large scale were contemplated. The French were looking for an opportunity to move against the Chemin des Dames, in the south, while we ourselves wanted to improve our position in front of Ypres by taking the Messines Ridge. It was essential, therefore, that the drive into the German line north and south of the Scarpe should carry all the signs of an attempt at a break-through, in order to compel the enemy to reinforce in that neighbourhood at the expense of other parts of his line. In addition to this, the operation gave the

British a chance of improving their position by the capture of important tactical features, such as Vimy Ridge and Monchy-le-Preux. If the tourist will stand under Vimy Ridge and imagine the Germans to be holding the top of the hill, he will realize that our position there was at one time anything but satisfactory. The enemy overlooked the whole of our lines, and made movement by daylight next to impossible.

Vimy Ridge.

The fight opened with an attack on Vimy Ridge. Just before dawn on 9th April, 1917, a racing snowstorm driving straight in their faces forced the German sentries to huddle under the scanty shelter of their parapets. It wasn't till a barrage joined the blizzard that they realized they were in for something more exciting that day than mere bad weather. Then alarm signals went up, telephones called out to the artillery, and the machine guns on the ridge opened on their night lines as the Canadians plodded their way to the assault through the mud. North of the ridge, across the Souchez Valley, the 73rd British Brigade co-operated by attacking the outposts covering Lens in the Bois-en-Hache.

The attack upon the Vimy Ridge on 9th April, 1917, was one of the most brilliantly executed operations of the war. Four divisions of Canadians attacked it in line, most of them attaining their first objectives with very few casualties, in spite of the exceptional difficulties of the country over which they had to advance, as the visitor will see at a glance.

Large numbers of Germans were captured in the great chalk excavations on the eastern side of

Daily Trips from Doullens

the Ridge, in which they had taken refuge during the barrage. These tunnels can still be seen; the largest of them are named the Volker and the Prince Arnault Tunnels respectively.

A walk along the crest of the Vimy Ridge will reveal to the tourist many things, principally, perhaps, the extent of the observation which was gained by its capture. The view from the crest is a truly astonishing one.

Lens to Oppy.

This attack threw the Germans back on their second line, which ran from Lens to Oppy. Lens itself would have fallen in the first bound had it not been for the mud and weather, which held up both men and guns. No Man's Land in those days was a veritable bog of shell holes, and the wonder is that our men ever got across it in that snowstorm in the half light, with the machine guns raking them from north and south. The first advance brought the infantry into Augres and Lievin. An aeroplane flying low over the hostile lines saw the enemy pulling back on Lens, and, dipping down towards our advanced posts, dropped a message to that effect. This was the signal for a general advance, which brought our outposts up to the outskirts of Lens. In the meantime efforts had been made to get guns and shells across No Man's Land. In many places the guns went up to their axles in the mud, while pack-mules with supplies sank slowly up to their girths. It was a trying and anxious time; ammunition was running short in the front line, and the German guns in their rear positions were getting troublesome. But the British gunners know how to overcome difficulties, and by nightfall they were across the sea of mud. If they were asked, they couldn't say how they did it. Brushwood and fascines had something to say to it, but the spirit of the artillery was really responsible for that victory over Nature. A good view of this battlefield can be obtained from the Lorette spur, which can be reached by the Bethune—Arras road. And then, when the tourist has taken in all the principal features of the landscape and recognized the original positions held by the opposing forces, it would be a good plan to walk across the battlefield via Angres and Lievin to Lens. Before the war these were flourishing mining towns, with smoking chimneys and busy thoroughfares. The German left them scrap-heaps of twisted iron and wrecked machinery mingling with the ruins of the miners' homes.

From Lens a walk across the ridge itself will cover most of the ground over which this battle raged, and on which a monument now stands as an everlasting tribute to those gallant sons of Canada whose battle cry meant terror and defeat to more than one German corps.

The Valley of the Scarpe.

The Arras road can be rejoined from the ridge, and the journey continued to the Valley of the Scarpe.

As soon as Vimy fell the pace quickened in front of Arras. As already stated, this battle was only a feint; but feints, when they fulfil their object, breed fierce and desperate fighting, and this one was no exception to the rule. The Germans were completely taken in by the determined advance of the British; the demoralizing atmosphere of a threatened break-through hung heavily

Official Photograph.] Hotel de Ville, Arras.

[*Official Photograph.*]

Scene in a Front Line Trench—Cleaning Lewis Gun.
(*Note the Fog Horn for Gas Alarm.*)

Daily Trips from Doullens

over the enemy lines, and for many days the eyes of the great General Staff were focussed on Arras and the heights along the Scarpe. Few battlefields have seen a more stubborn defence and more violent counter-attacks. Monchy-le-Preux, Rœux, Gavrelle, and Greenland Hill changed hands more than once; in fact, it may be said that both sides were fought to a standstill, until in the end the Germans were forced to withdraw twelve of their best divisions, exhausted, from the field. British doggedness told in the long run, and the offensive fulfilled the part designed for it in the Allied plan. Here is, indeed, a soldier's battlefield, and it is worth more than a passing visit.

Arras.

Arras itself—the ancient capital of Artois—is well worth a visit. Traces of Spanish rule may still be seen in the older houses with their quaint roofs and windows. Arras, like Amiens, came in for its share of the scars of war; it is one of the brave old towns of France. The city abounded with cellars and underground passages, and prior to the great battle British engineers were hard at work for many months connecting these up as a means of subterranean advance for the attacking troops. These were eventually lit by electric light, water was pumped into them by pipe lines, and a small tramway was in full working order. It was found possible to concentrate three whole divisions of infantry, concealed from view, in this manner, and the great problem of forming up a big attack in this sector—a problem which had been previously tackled unsuccessfully by the French in 1915—was solved.

The Battle of Arras will go down to history as

an outstanding example of immense difficulties cleverly overcome by preparation, patience, and skilful field engineering.

By moving on from St. Pol or Doullens the tourist will be well placed for visiting the old line between Arras and Thiepval, including Gommecourt and the trenches in the vicinity of Hannescamps and Fonquevillers. Although, with the exception of Gommecourt, no important battle was fought there, it will nevertheless be full of interest, and will doubtless hold many sacred spots for some.

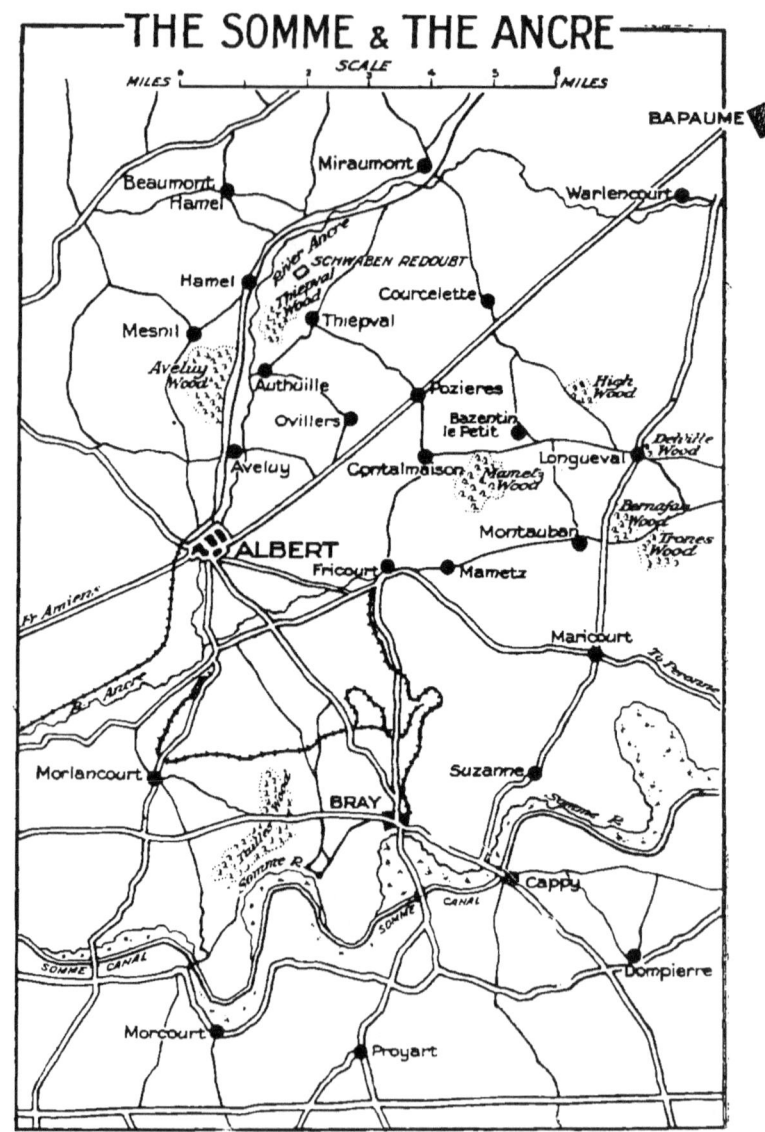

CHAPTER VIII

DAILY TRIPS FROM AMIENS: A DAY AT THIEPVAL, BEAUMONT-HAMEL, AND THE BATTLEFIELDS OF THE ANCRE—THE SOMME, FRICOURT, MAMETZ, MONTAUBAN, AND LONGUEVAL— THE WOODS OF THE SOMME: BERNAFAY, MAMETZ, TRONES, DELVILLE, AND THE BOIS DE FOURNEAUX.

A Day at Thiepval, Beaumont-Hamel, and the Battlefields of the Ancre.

THE first time I saw the Somme country was in August, 1915, when the division with which I was serving, shattered and exhausted after the second Battle of Ypres, was moved southwards to take over a large sector of trenches from the French. The change from the Ypres Salient was a welcome one, especially when it was discovered that the new sector was what the soldier terms "cushy." There had been practically no severe fighting in this country. The villages of Beaumont-Hamel, Ovillers, Fricourt, and Mametz, on the German side of the lines, looked fresh and smiling in the beautiful summer weather; while on our side places such as Mailly-Mailly, Acheux, Mesnil, Albert, and Bray, all of which were very close to the front trenches, were almost untouched and still inhabited by their civilian population. The River Ancre pursued its peaceful course, contributing fish to friend and foe alike (indeed, it was no uncommon sight to observe men quietly fishing within a few yards of the Germans, their only protection being a few strands of rusty barbed wire). The woods of Aveluy, Thiepval, Mametz, Bernafay, Delville, and Trones were filled with birds and rabbits. In fact, the whole sector was a rest cure, and the British divisions which arrived to inhabit it lifted up voices of thankfulness, and proceeded to lick their wounds and be happy for a season. Little did they dream that this peaceful country was to become the scene of battles as desperate as any which had been experienced in the Ypres Salient, or anywhere else ; that the names of those smiling villages would go down to history with stories of the terrific fighting with which they were to be associated ; that that clear, beautiful little river would one day be choked with corpses and dyed with blood ; that those shady, peaceful woods would be withered away until they became a ghastly scene of shell-shattered stumps. Yet so it happened !

From Amiens to Thiepval is twenty and a half miles by road, and over rough country, but the visitor will save much time by taking a train to **Albert**, and walking the remainder of the distance. The reason why a visit to Thiepval is advised in particular, when the whole neighbourhood teems with places of equal interest, is that the hill and village of this name were what is known in military language as " key positions," by reason of the fact that here the ground in German possession sloped upwards to strongly fortified positions, behind which was a ridge, giving excellent observation of the surrounding country for miles, and from which German guns could sweep the whole approaches to the position. The visitor, from Thiepval village, will be able to see at a glance the

Daily Trips from Amiens

nature of the task which was undertaken by the British on the 1st July, 1916; he will still be able to study the remnants of the wonderful field defences which came so near to defeating the whole effort, and which inflicted such severe casualties upon the attackers. This little book can lay no claim to be a history, but by recommending its reader to walk from Thiepval to Pozières (sacred to the valour of many thousands of Australians), and from Pozières back to Albert, it may claim to have helped him to understand perhaps a small part of one of the bitterest struggles in the world's history. In this small triangle lie the villages of Aveluy, Authuille, Ovillers, and the Leipzig Redoubt, while to the north-east of Thiepval from the ruins of the famous Schwaben Redoubt can be seen the course of the River Ancre as it runs southwards to join the Somme, and the marvellous stronghold of Beaumont-Hamel.

With the defences of Beaumont-Hamel are associated the wonderful tunnels and excavations of the Ravine-en-Y, in which the Germans, by immense energy and industry, constructed huge dugouts and tunnels capable of safely sheltering many thousands of men, and from which they were able to reinforce almost any part of this neighbourhood which was attacked from the west. It was not until the heights of Thiepval and the Schwaben Redoubt had been captured by the British in November, 1916, that Beaumont-Hamel could be attacked with any certainty of success, and it will be remembered that this attack was eventually launched by the Naval Division in a heavy snowstorm in that month, the river crossed under unimaginable difficulties, and Beaumont-Hamel and the Ravine-en-Y were captured. For the personal

direction and leading of this glorious effort, Brigadier-General Freyberg was granted the V.C., and the fame of the Naval Division was noised abroad.

The Somme, Fricourt, Mametz, Montauban, and Longueval.

Again taking Albert as a starting point, our visitor may profitably spend a day in viewing the country, this time to its immediate south. The road from Albert to Fricourt, some three miles, can be described as the main channel of communication to the Battle of the Somme. The villages of Fricourt and Mametz, both strongly defended, fell to the British on the first day of the July, 1916, fighting, and so enabled this road to be used for reinforcements and supplies, and it can be said with truth that, as the fighting progressed, nearly every division in the Army passed the forlorn cemetery at Fricourt, which seemed to be the last link with the outside world. From here the visitor may take the northward road to Contalmaison, and then strike east to Longueval, or he may climb the small hill to Mametz and continue his journey to Montauban. Whichever way he may choose, the course of the fighting can be easily followed. From Contalmaison he will see the heights of Pozières and the ruins of Bazentin-le-Petit, while from Montauban a magnificent view of Longueval and the country to the east as far as Ginchy can be obtained. It is no exaggeration to state that practically every yard of this country was the scene of fighting of the most stubborn description during 1916, and it was only by the dogged pressure which was maintained so continuously, driving the enemy from wood to wood and from village to village until Le Transloy was reached, that the

Daily Trips from Amiens

Germans were obliged to evacuate their whole line and retire upon the Hindenburg positions many miles to the east.

The Woods of the Somme—Bernafay, Mametz, Trones, Delville, and the Bois de Fourneaux.

Wood fighting has always been associated, as far as the general public is concerned, with the romantic side of war; Red Indians crawling through the thick undergrowth and signalling to each other by cries in imitation of the cries of birds are largely responsible for this; or the crafty scout disguised as a holly bush stealthily making his reconnaissance and blazing his lonely trail from tree to tree may have a share in it too. But nothing could be more withering to the real spirit of romance in war than the wood fighting which took place during the initial stages of the Battle of the Somme in 1916. It was ghastly, and no other word in the dictionary can adequately describe it.

The German second line positions ran through Mametz, Bernafay, and Trones Woods, and very excellently planned positions they were. Well-concealed trenches and strong points with good communications to the rear were numerous, while observation of the attacking troops was obtained by means of crows' nests skilfully constructed in the highest trees. At first, so great had been the initial success of the first great attack in this neighbourhood, it was thought that these woods would be undefended, and battalions coming up full of zeal and enthusiasm to exploit the triumph advanced right into them. Few returned, except in a shattered condition. More battalions advanced, this time full of the purpose to attack, but attack after attack was repulsed. It was then decided to shell these woods heavily, which was done; the Germans retiring by means of their rear communication trenches until the shelling was over, returned at once, and repelled further attacks in the same way as before. This happened many times, the only appreciable result being that the woods were becoming gradually thinner and the thick undergrowth entirely blasted away. In Mametz Wood the 38th Welsh Division was almost annihilated before it eventually established itself; in Trones and Bernafay Woods battalion after battalion literally disappeared. But perhaps the two most famous woods were Delville and the Bois de Fourneaux or High Wood. In both of these the British, after immense effort, managed to establish positions close up to the German strong points. Then began a type of hand-to-hand fighting with bomb and bayonet which lasted for months without any material advantage being gained by either side. The casualties, both British and German, were very high, and gradually the woods themselves simply disappeared under the concentrated shell fire of both sides. All that remains of them now is a series of battered tree-trunks, which can best be described as monuments to the numerous graves which surround them. The visitor should survey the scene with the reverence which it deserves.

Official Photographs.]
1. **A Huge Shell Crater in Mametz Wood.**   2. **Remains of a Machine Gun Platform in a Tree.**

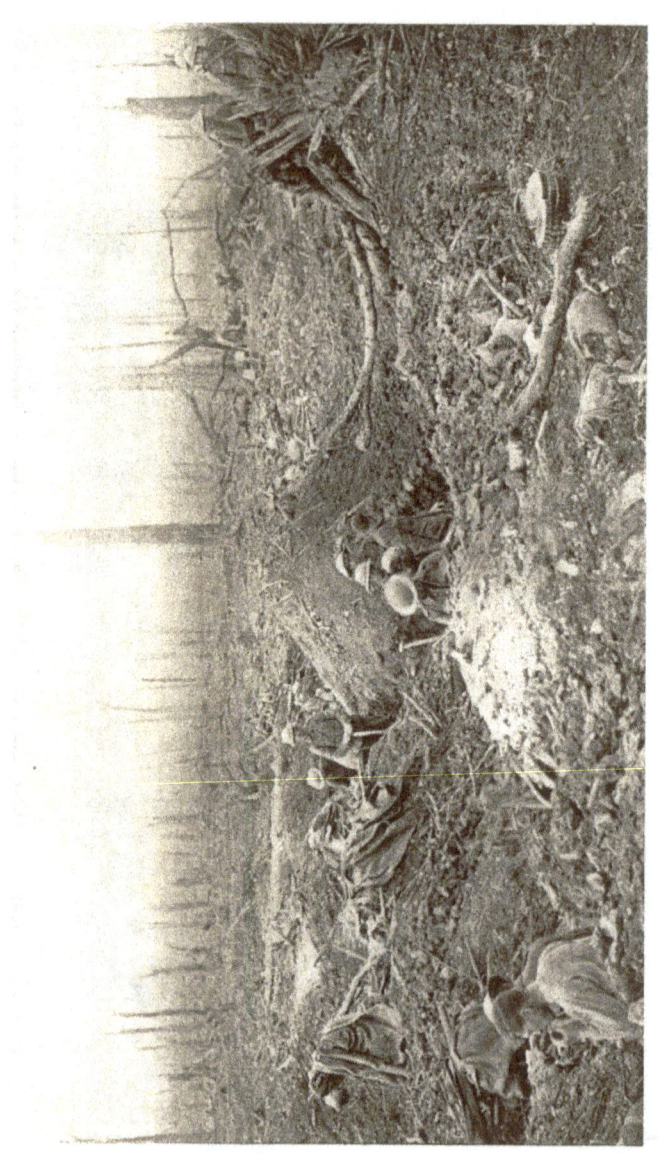

Official Photograph.] **A Communication Trench through a Wood.**
The name of the Wood does not matter, all the woods of the Somme are in much the same condition

CHAPTER IX

THE SCENES OF THE BRITISH RETREAT IN MARCH 1918: THE MOST CRITICAL DAY OF THE WAR—THE THIN KHAKI LINE—GERMAN LUCK—A FIGHTING RETREAT—AMIENS THE BEST HEADQUARTERS—THE LONG, STRAIGHT ROAD

The Most Critical Day of the War.

"*At about 8 a.m. this morning, after an intense bombardment of both high explosives and gas shells on forward positions and back areas, a powerful infantry attack was launched by the enemy on a front of over fifty miles, extending from the River Oise, in the neighbourhood of La Fere, to the Sensee River about Croiselles. Hostile artillery demonstrations have taken place on a wide front north of La Bassée Canal and in the Ypres sector. The attack, which for some time past was known to be in course of preparation, has been pressed with the greatest vigour and determination throughout the day.*"—OFFICIAL COMMUNIQUE, MARCH 21st, 1918.

"The Kaiser's Battle!" "All Germany marching to Victory!" "We will force the British to make Peace!" So ran the exultant headings in the German newspapers, to be copied only too quickly by many of our own, until the mailed fist of her enemies was shaking and rattling throughout the British Empire, and the timid and fainthearted quailed and knelt before it. Then came the news from the front: the sudden appearance of the gilded youth, dressed in the apparel of a

48 The Western Battlefields

Staff Officer, arriving in crowded London hotels with premature news of crushing defeat; of the panic of the camp-followers in France; of the wild rush of the Italian road-menders through Amiens; of the terror-stricken flight of the Chinese Labour units; of the awful straggling processions of weary refugees. Such was the effect of the German attack in front of St. Quentin on March 21st, 1918.

The Thin Khaki Line.

But it is well to recollect the thin khaki lines of British troops "standing-to" in their battle positions at 5.30 a.m., under the most terrific bombardment which had ever been known in the history of war, peering through the dense mist, and waiting—the advanced troops waiting in the certain knowledge of annihilation and death.

A breathless messenger on a red-hot motor bicycle arrives at the headquarters of the Fifth Army :—" The artillery duel is terrific, particularly in the region of the ridges about St. Quentin, which appear to be the main objective of the German scheme," reads his message, and in time this proved to be only too true. A gap had been made in the line, and through this gap the German hordes were pouring in a manner which proved that only by a retreat, and that upon a vast scale, could the situation be saved.

But they would have held them, those thin khaki lines—every single division of the Fifth Army would have held in their selected battle positions, had it not been for that confounded mist! There are many competent authorities who believe that General Gough's scheme of defence in depth was sound, that his dispositions with the number of troops at his disposal were wisely and

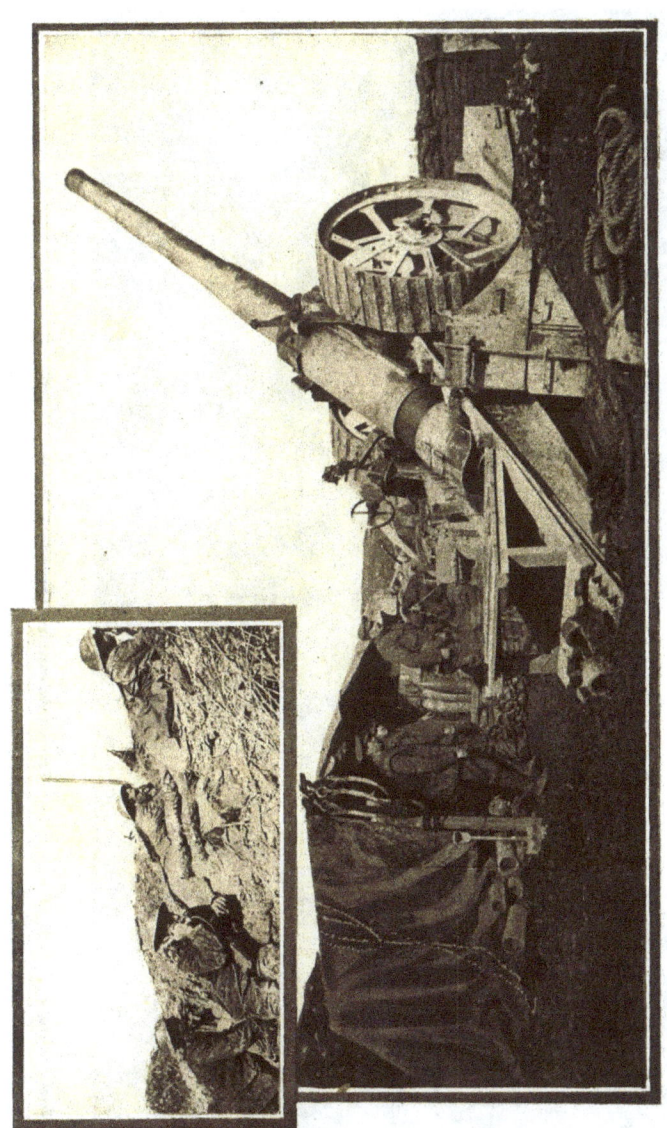

Official Photographs.
1. Forward Observation Officer engaged in "Registering" on Prominent Features of the Enemy's Line.
2. A High Velocity Naval Gun ready to Fire.

Official Photograph.] Troops Advancing through a Ruined Town.

Scenes from British Retreat, 1918

correctly planned, and that every possible military precaution had been taken and studied, and every possible situation prepared for—except that mist!

A visit to one or more of these positions will convince the tourist that the defensive measures adopted by the Fifth Army were as complete and perfect as the strength of the troops and the ground permitted. Writers have already been busy with this chapter of the war, and more will probably be said on the subject. It has already been hinted that the attack came as a surprise, and that proper defensive measures were not in force to deal with a break through on a large scale. But those who fought in this great battle can tell a different story. The real trouble was that the troops were strung out over too long a line, making it impossible to hold the position in that strength and depth which would have broken up an attack and opened the way for a counter-attack. Even as it was the German calculations missed badly, and on the morning of the second day the enemy was many miles east of the line he was timed to reach.

German Luck.

The Germans had a reputation for good fortune with regard to weather conditions, but never had they such extraordinary good luck as on the morning of March 21st, 1918. The morning of the 20th, the day before, had broken bright and cloudless; if they had attacked that day they would have been defeated in their initial stage, in spite of the fact that they had an average of one gun to every twelve or fifteen yards, besides great numbers of trench mortars, which were used

to cut the wire on our forward positions ; in spite of the fact that they threw in nine divisions of infantry on a front of less than 12,000 yards at St. Quentin alone.

But the mist of the morning of the 21st altered everything. Our troops in the advanced trenches saw nothing of their enemy until he was trampling over them ; our supports in their battle positions behind did not even know that their comrades in the forward positions had come into action until the Germans were upon them ; machine guns in magnificent defensive positions were unable to fire, fearing to shoot their own infantry, and unable to distinguish friend from foe ; field guns—those of them that remained after the enemy's bombardment, which had annihilated most of them—could only fire on their old barrage lines until the enemy was sweeping round them. Truly it was a lucky mist for Germany!

A Fighting Retreat.

German infantry were up against our wire before they were discovered. Some had even succeeded in passing round the flanks of the positions. This was how the gaps were made, and through these gaps the Germans poured their reserves. Rockets and Véry lights, fired by their leading troops, guided them. This penetration which took place at nearly every position under cover of the fog, allowed the enemy to surround our posts, and the British found themselves attacked on all sides. All round fighting became the order of the day, and while this was going on fresh troops were pushed through to the rearmost British lines. Still the fighting continued ; in front counter-attacks and gallant assaults were made by small

Scenes from British Retreat, 1918

bodies of our infantry against overpowering and ever-increasing bodies of Germans. The enemy felt uneasy about these little nests of British. They were spoiling their advance, losing them valuable time, and making it difficult to get forward. There was a danger, too, that British reserves might arrive on the scene at any moment and counter-attack them while they were disorganized. Fortunately for them, however, no British reserves were at hand, and they were free to take on these little posts and endeavour to capture or wipe them out. For the British commander the situation called for a quick decision. He had no big force with which to deliver a counter-stroke, and thus relieve his sorely tried troops. He had only two courses open to him—to order his troops to stand where they were and fight it out, or to withdraw his troops and give ground to the enemy. He naturally decided on the latter, for if he had ordered a fight to a finish, he would have given the Germans the men as well as the ground.

The Fifth Army withdrew fighting, and did it so skilfully that the main body got clear without the Germans knowing it. A rearguard action was fought back to the line of the Somme, and finally to the outposts in front of Amiens. Desperate fighting took place at Chaulnes, Pusieux, and Dreslincourt. The Germans soon discovered that in spite of their superior strength and the extravagant use of fresh troops the tired British Army had more than one kick left in it, and could still launch those telling counter-attacks, which had such a demoralizing effect on their men.

The Western Battlefields

Amiens the Best Headquarters.

Amiens, the gateway to the battlefields of the Somme, stands on the edge of that devastated region over which the tide of war ebbed and flowed for four long years. This fine old cathedral town, the ancient capital of Picardy, is well supplied, as has been mentioned, with comfortable hotels and restaurants. It is within easy reach of the coast by rail, and is on the main line between Boulogne and Paris. Motors can be hired at reasonable rates, and the tourist will find both officials and citizens courteous and kind and anxious to help. It is an ideal headquarters for those who want to visit the ground over which the British fell back in face of the great German drive of March, 1918.

The 5th British Army held a line of trenches in front of St. Quentin. The positions included Vendhuile, the high ground east of Roussoy, and Le Verguier. Further south the line ran through Pontruet and west of St. Quentin. The German line kept west of the St. Quentin Canal, and was roughly parallel to the British. Bony-Bellicourt and St. Quentin itself were in German hands. This area was the storm centre of the battle of the 21st March, 1918.

For many days before the "crash" it was evident that something unusual was taking place behind the enemy lines. In fact, it was very clear that an offensive on a large scale was in contemplation. Air reconnaissances reported the construction of bridges at various places over the St. Quentin Canal; infantry observers noticed the presence of German officers scanning the British trenches from their own forward posts; and although enemy documents captured later con-

Official Photograph. **A Tank in Difficulties.**

Official Photographs.]
 1. Cologne as seen from an Aeroplane.
 2. Victory! The British Occupation of Cologne.
 3. Tanks in Review Order outside Cologne Cathedral.

Scenes from British Retreat, 1918

tained strict instructions as to secrecy and deception, in the plans and preparations for the battle the British Intelligence Service was able to fix the attack almost to the day. A raid into the enemy lines on the night before the assault, resulting in the capture of some Germans, put any remaining doubts on the subject at rest. So it was no surprise to the troops of the Fifth Army when the storm burst on the early morning of March 21st, and the German guns put down their barrage on our lines. In addition to the front line system, our defences consisted of supporting posts on the high ground at Lempire, Roussoy, Hargicourt, Le Vergier, and Maissemy; while, in rear of these, other positions were held at Epéhy, Templeux, Hervilly, and Vendelles. The rear positions were allotted to troops resting in reserve, and were manned as soon as the attack developed.

The Long, Straight Road.

The long, straight road from Amiens to St. Quentin, crossing the Somme at Brie, will take the tourist to the most interesting scenes of this great retreat. From St. Quentin the original British front line can be visited, and then the rearguards might be followed step by step back to Villers Bretonneux, where the tourist would be well advised to spend a day wandering round that famous battlefield and the positions in its vicinity. And then—a little way back on the homeward journey the slender spire of the old cathedral comes into view, and one wonders how Amiens managed to escape the fate of Ypres.

It may be as well to mention here that, although the battlefields have been taken from north to

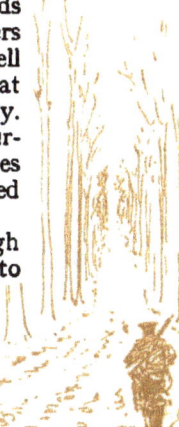

south, there is no reason why the tourist should not work his way from south to north, making Amiens his first headquarters, and finishing up at Ypres or Ostend. There is one point, however, which should not be overlooked. The trips from Amiens in most cases involve long journeys, and the more daylight one can get for these the better; whereas the trips from centres like Lille and Ypres are not so long. So a great deal will depend on the time of year whether the tourist will work from north to south or *vice versa*. The moon, too, may play no small part in the pilgrim's plans. A battlefield or an old trench line or an old billet, when viewed by moonlight, will bring back old times and old scenes which fail to grip in the light of day. Besides this, a bright night for the long journey home is not to be despised.

CHAPTER X

From Trenches to War in the Open—The Hundred Days' Battle — Fighting in the Industrial Districts of Belgium— Armistice — Waterloo Revisited — An Interesting Comparison.

The Change to Open Warfare.

If the greater part of this little book has been devoted to the places with which the prolonged period of trench warfare was associated on the Western Front, it is because the majority of the vast throng of persons who journeyed to and fro between England and France or Belgium during the Great War participated in that period. But the beginning and the end of this world's conflict will probably go down to posterity as the most interesting parts of it, chiefly because of the extraordinary amount of movement which took place in the opening and closing stages. And movement has been described as the soul of war, bringing out qualities of leadership and initiative in the commander, and endurance and stubborn purpose in the troops, which can never be gained during periods of comparative stagnation.

The change from months and months of continuous trench warfare to mobile fighting in the open was a sudden one for the British Army, and the difficulties involved may be hard to understand by civilian readers. It must be explained, therefore, that in trench warfare everything

The Western Battlefields

is of a routine nature. There is a definite line of enemy trenches, the position of which is known to the opposing army by means of aeroplane photographs and information received from patrols. There is a defined and known track of country called No Man's Land, separating the two systems of trenches, and upon which the guns of both sides are laid. There are definite communication trenches, definite dug-outs for commanders, definite systems of telephone communication; in fact, everything is "cut and dried," even to the positions of sentries and sentry groups. Rations come up at night by the same routes and arrive at the same time; ammunition dumps remain in the same places and are refilled as required. Everything is organized with a view to rigid defence. To change from warfare of this nature suddenly and advance in pursuit of an enemy whose positions and intentions are unknown is one of the most difficult operations in war, yet many divisions of the army accomplished this with conspicuous success.

The Hundred Days' Battle.

From the first week of August, 1918, the British Army began to advance on almost every part of the front, and from that week it can be said that its victorious progress never stopped until the day the Armistice was signed. To describe an advance of this nature in detail is impossible, while to attempt to guide a visitor to the outstanding places of interest during it would be equally so. The whole battle lasted over one hundred days, and in it were engaged the largest number of troops ever concentrated in a single battle, the battlefield lying between Switzerland

From Trenches to Open Warfare   57

and the sea. But there are two impressions of this battle which a visitor may obtain, and which if time permits he ought to obtain. One is to follow the line of the advance from Ypres to Courtrai, and to examine the immense difficulties of fighting in a highly populated industrial country; the other is to take train from Lille to Brussels, and to revisit the field of Waterloo, in the knowledge that this hallowed spot was the scene of England's greatness at the two greatest crises of her history. For in October, 1918, British cavalry were actually in action on the battlefield where the Duke of Wellington routed Napoleon's Grand Army in 1815.

Fighting in the Industrial Districts of Belgium.

The journey from Ypres to Courtrai may now be made by train for a few francs. The line runs through the town of Menin, and the country on every side teems with interest, for it was in this neighbourhood, and as far north as Roulers, that the Germans made a desperate stand to delay the great outflanking movement of the armies under the King of the Belgians, using every little hill and tactical feature of the country to fight rearguard actions with light artillery and machine guns. Stubborn fighting also took place in the town of Courtrai, through which runs the River Lys; and the story of how the British established pontoon bridges across this river under heavy fire, and captured the town by fighting from street to street, is a romantic one. With the capture of Courtrai and Lille practically the whole of the industrial part of Northern France and Belgium fell into our hands, and the war was won.

The Western Battlefields

Waterloo Revisited.

To visit the field of Waterloo nowadays may seem an unnecessary kind of amusement, when there are so many modern battlefields to engross one's attention; nevertheless the visitor is advised to go there with an object which will be presently explained. The road from Brussels to Waterloo is a very wide and beautiful one, with numerous places of historical interest by the way, and from the very start the imagination is gripped by the thought of the great drama which was enacted upon it a century ago. How extraordinarily easy to visualize the scenes of "Vanity Fair"—the galloping horsemen hurrying from the great ball at Brussels at break-neck pace; the mad crowd of cowardly fugitives returning at the sound of the first discharge, to spread rumours of alarm and despondency in the rear (perhaps the visitor will have some knowledge of such happenings in the late campaign, and of what the confusion of camp-followers is really like), the wild ride of Lady Smith, of the Rifle Brigade, when she rode out to search for the body of her husband, Sir Harry Smith, who they told her had been killed in the battle, and whom she eventually found safe and well, marching with his battalion, after she had braved terrors unspeakable in the field! These things become a reality, and a thrill of excitement will be felt when the foot of the Lion Monument is reached, a monument erected by the Allied Powers as a symbol of victory. From the summit of the Lion Monument the best panoramic view of the battlefield of Waterloo can be obtained; there are 226 steps to be climbed before the summit is

An Interesting Comparison

reached, and to do it without a stop is an interesting test of physical training. Carved upon the unfortunate lion the visitor will see thousands of the numbers, names and regiments of British soldiers who had been given leave to visit Waterloo after the Armistice, and to whom the scene of their ancestors' triumph probably caused little emotion. But the "Tommy" of 1914 to 1918 was just the same sort of fellow as the thousands of gallant fellows who died on the field of Waterloo that England might live—perhaps even a finer fellow, because, although they were both countlessly outnumbered by their enemies, as the British Army invariably seems to be, the heroes of Waterloo had a better fight for their money.

An Interesting Comparison.

And that is precisely the reason why the visitor is advised to see this spot as the final item of his tour—to compare in his mind the fighting of Waterloo with the fighting of the Great War. In all but principle he will find there is nothing the same. When you descend the monument you proceed to a little rotunda building, where you stand on a platform in the centre of a huge circular picture representing the battle of Waterloo. There you see French cavalry charging British squares of red and green coated infantry, while their own infantry manœuvre into position in dense masses behind. In the far distance is Napoleon, seated on a white horse, with glittering staff around him; and in the far distance on the Allied side you can see the Iron Duke similarly situated. During the Great War it was a common thing to hear fellows wishing

they had been born a century earlier, because fighting must have been rather fun then, but I don't know that I agree. The thought of being charged by cavalry in the open was always a nightmare; I can't imagine anything worse from an infantryman's point of view, and in this way barbed wire had its advantages. Also there were few field ambulances in Wellington's army, and the casualties at Waterloo were over 20,000!

Marshal Foch is said to have stated that there are only two studies of vital importance to a soldier's career—first, the history of past campaigns; and, second, the psychology of great leaders. He must be right, for there is nothing new to-day in the tactics of war, and nothing different in our traditional leadership by brave men; only the conditions have changed, and the red coats, and the ambulances. The unconquerable spirit of the British soldier is just the same.

CONCLUSION

THE SENTINELS.

The little crosses on the hillside mark the rest billets of our comrades of the trenches. They haven't really left us; they are only on ahead, like scouts, finding out the way. One day we will join them, and then they will guide us over "No Man's Land" into that friendly country of peace and rest and happiness. Meanwhile, they stand on guard along the battle front. Let us not forget.

GALE & POLDEN, LIMITED

Medals and Ribbons of the British Army

(Revised and up-to-date edition). A handsome plate, size 27½in. by 18½in. in colours, showing all medals both sides (from the year 1800 to present day), together with ribbons in correct colours and clasps. Forms a complete record in Medals of the Battles of the British Empire during the past 120 years, and is of special interest now, as it shows the War Decorations bestowed on British Officers and Men by the British, French, and Russian Governments in the last campaign **1s. 6d.**

Commemoration Banners in Honour of the Heroic Deeds of the First Seven Divisions from Mons to Ypres, 1914

Dedicated at the Royal Albert Hall, London, W., Saturday, December 15th, 1917, at a Choral Celebration which Their Majesties attended. These Banners are now distributed among the various Cathedrals, Churches, etc., throughout the British Isles. Full list of the Series of these Reproductions sent upon application. Correctly reproduced from the original banners, and beautifully printed in full colours on Fine Art Paper, mounted on hand-made card, plate-marked, with printed title. Suitable for framing. Each (by post, 1/3) **1s.**

Cavalry Standards, Guidons, and Drum Banners of the British Army

A handsome plate, size 20in. by 30in., containing 44 designs, folding into artistic covers. The reproduction in actual colours of these beautiful crimson silk standards and guidons, also the gorgeous silk drum banners, is a triumph of British Colour Printing. The wealth of intricate embroideries is faithfully reproduced, showing the crests surrounded by wreaths of battle honours. **1s. 6d.**

2 AMEN CORNER, LONDON, E.C. 4
Or of all Booksellers

GALE & POLDEN, LIMITED

Crests & Badges of the British Army

Size 34in. by 22in. Beautifully illustrated in gold and colours, forming a complete record of the Crests of the Army. A real work of art. The Crest of every Regiment in the Regular Army: Cavalry, Artillery, Infantry, etc., is shown, correct in all details, and with the correct titles attached. Can be supplied either in book form or flat for framing. **1s.6d.**

Colours of Infantry Regiments of the British Army

These handsome sheets, size 20in. by 30in., each contains 40 sets of Colours of the Regiments of Foot Guards and Infantry of the Line, faithfully reproduced in beautiful colours. Correct in every detail. As very few of our soldiers of to-day have even seen the Colours of their own Regiment, these sheets will prove of deep interest to them. This collection makes a gorgeous display of unending interest, and is a fine example of British Colour Printing. SHEET 1 contains the Colours of the 5 Regiments of Foot Guards and Infantry up to those of the Hampshire Regiment. SHEET 2 contains the Regimental Colours of the Rest of the Infantry Regiments, together with those of the Royal Marines, Royal Military College, etc. **1s.6d.**

Regimental Ribbons and Buttons of the British Army

Issued in one sheet, 33½in. by 21in. Lithographed in Colours; correct reproduction of silk ribbons and regimental crested buttons. 116 designs, showing the correct Buttons of every Regiment in the British Army, with their Regimental Ribbons in Colours. Bound in handsome covers **1s.6d.**

Regimental Nicknames and Traditions of the British Army

This unique book describes briefly, but clearly, the history, uniform, battle honours, traditions, nicknames, and crest of every Regiment in the British Army, and is profusely illustrated with 32 coloured plates. The many peculiarities of dress and custom in the Army are touched on, and the whole forms a reliable book of reference. In stiff covers, 118 pages of text **2s.**

2 AMEN CORNER, LONDON, E.C. 4
Or of all Booksellers

Solid Silver Keyless Lever Watch, Fully Jewelled, Mounted on Suède Straps

£5 0 0

BRACELET WATCHES

THE Goldsmiths & Silversmiths Company maintain a comprehensive stock of Wristlet Watches in Gold and Solid Silver of finest quality and representing the best value obtainable.

An Illustrated Catalogue will be sent, post free, on application.

THE GOLDSMITHS & SILVERSMITHS COMPANY L^{TD}.. *with which is incorporated The Goldsmiths Alliance L^d. Est^d 1751.*

Jewellers to His Majesty the King

112 REGENT STREET, LONDON, W. 1

NAVAL & MILITARY PRESS

GUIDES TO THE ALLIED LINE AND MEMORIALS ON THE WESTERN FRONT

Works such as these N&MP productions formed the 'Roots of Remembrance' that 100+ years on still attract pilgrims in their droves to visit the Western front and its memorials to the fallen

THEY ARE ALWAYS IN PRINT AND ALWAYS AVAILABLE

Definitely books to add to your backpack when taking a pilgrimage to France, and have a seasoned veteran or expert vividly describe the action or memorial

A GUIDE TO THE AMERICAN WW1 BATTLEFIELDS OF EUROPE
Prepared by the American Battle Monuments Commission

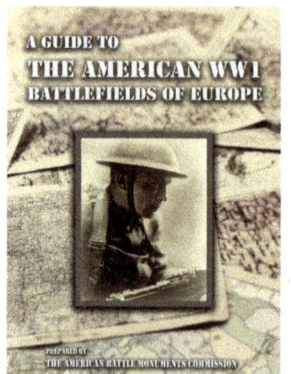

A solid reference for those who wish to know about the American evolvement in the Great War, and also good for family members discovering where a doughboy great-grandfather fought – this classic is a good place to start. This 1927 guide is organised by region and campaign: Aisne-Marne, St. Mihel, Meuse-Argonne, Champagne, and the areas north of Paris including Flanders, Ypres, the St. Quentin Canal Tunnel and Cantigny. It includes narrative, photographs and maps.

9781474540483

BRITISH MEMORIALS OF THE GREAT WAR

A historical and attractive guide to the various national, regimental and divisional memorials on the Western Front, with photographs and maps, and also notes on memorials further afield including Gallipoli. Published in the 1930s by pioneer travel agency and printing company Dean & Dawson, who conducted battlefield visits. An interesting contemporary tour prospectus is reprinted with this book that outlines the various tours to the Somme, Ypres, Arras etc, along with the maps that accompanied the original publication.

9781474537995

GOOD-BYE TO THE BATTLEFIELDS
Today and Yesterday on the Western Front

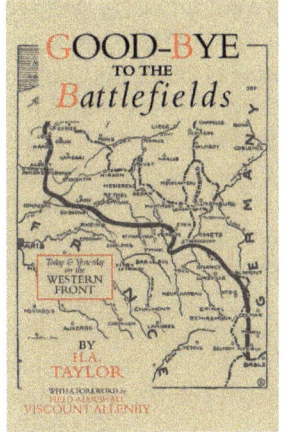

Captain Taylor walks the battlefields of the Western Front 'as they are today (1928)', with good descriptions of the battlefields, relics and memorials during the inter-war period, along with 1920s photographs of towns and villages, cemeteries, memorials and battlefield areas during the period of post-war reconstruction.

With his reminiscences of events, that lend a real atmosphere, his memory and feet "follow our khaki-clad columns moving northward". This is definitely one book to add to your backpack when taking a pilgrimage to France.

9781474536967

PILGRIM'S GUIDE TO THE YPRES SALIENT

One of the earliest guidebooks to the Ypres Salient, stated by the author to be compiled for the ex-servicemen who may wish to visit the graves and battlefields of the Great War. Unusually, and interestingly, it includes essays on various aspects of service in the Salient: Hugh Pollard on infantry, Walter Gardiner on mining, F. Worthington on RAMC Work; Machine Guns in the Salient by 'Maxim', etc.

9781474536738

TWENTY YEARS AFTER - THE BATTLEFIELDS OF 1914-1918 THEN & NOW THREE VOLUME SET

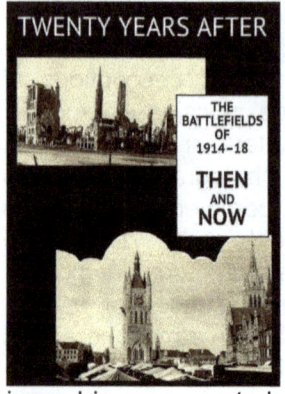

'Twenty Years After – The Battlefields of 1914-1918 Then & Now' is not a publishing curiosity but a fascinating piece of Great War history that is still of much value today.

Alongside the atmospheric images is an extensive text, describing many operations and locations on all Fronts, but mainly France & Flanders. With its thousands of superb photographs, this is a fine reference work that was originally issued in many parts but now much more convenient in this bound form.

9781783315505

GUIDE TO THE WAR REGIONS OF FRANCE AND BELGIUM
With the Best Routes & Chief Features of Interest

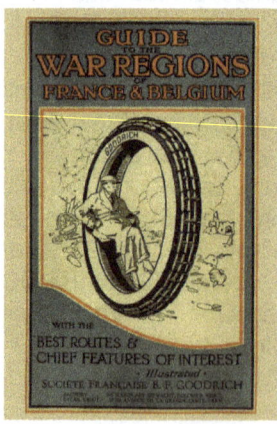

Published in the 1920s by Goodrich tyre company, 'Guide to the War Regions of France & Belgium' was aimed at the relatively new phenomenon and the independent motorist. Packed with useful information including coloured maps, photographs, together with advice for motorists and details of seventeen different war regions, each with map, route, hotels, historical and economic accounts, a short history of the operations and war facts.

These war regions include: The Marne, Champagne, Verdun, Nancy, Vosges, Alsace, Lorraine, Ardennes, Belgium, Yser,

Artois, Picardy, Chemin-des-Dames, Somme, Cambrai, Arras and Ypres. Unlike our reprint of 'The White Cross Touring Atlas of the Western Battlefields' that is concerned with visiting the war graves of the fallen, this guide is angled towards the battlefield tourist.

9781783319473

THE WHITE CROSS TOURING ATLAS OF THE WESTERN BATTLEFIELDS

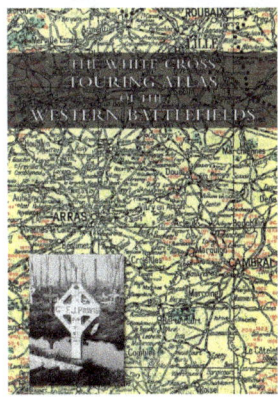

An early historical Great War battlefield guide the whole Western Front, complete with 64 good colour maps, a descriptive text and a War Graves Index of over 1700 cemeteries. The main value to this book, that is now very scarce in it's original printing, is that it shows the locations of many of the British cemeteries that were later consolidated by the CWG.

9781783315758

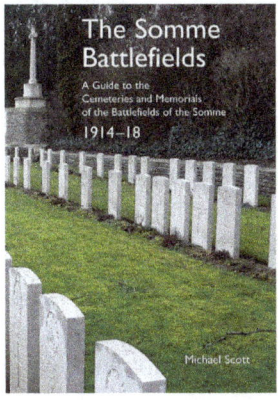

SOMME BATTLEFIELDS
A Guide to the Cemeteries and Memorials of the Battlefields of the Somme 1914-18

An introduction to the battlefields of the Somme through the cemeteries and the memorials. Every cemetery within which is buried a man recorded by the CWGC is covered. The story of the cemetery, the local memorials and information of the lives and war experiences of some of those buried in each cemetery is told.

9781783312900

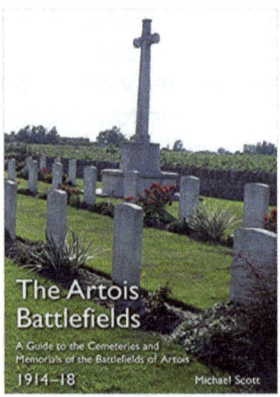

ARTOIS BATTLEFIELDS
A Guide to the Cemeteries and Memorials of the Battlefields of Artois 1914–18

This introduction to the battlefields of Artois is told through the war cemeteries and those buried within. The story of the cemetery, local memorials and lives and war experiences of some of those buried in each cemetery are covered.

9781783314768

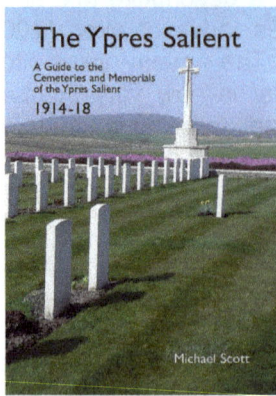

YPRES SALIENT
A Guide to the Cemeteries and Memorials of the Ypres Salient 1914-18

An exciting new version of an earlier work, this introduction to the battlefields of the Ypres Salient is through the cemeteries and those buried within. The story of the cemetery, local memorials and lives and war experiences of some of those buried in each cemetery is told.   **9781783313518**

SILENT CITIES
An illustrated guide to the war Cemeteries & Memorials to the missing in France & Flanders 1914-1918

The classic guide to the War Cemeteries in France and Flanders. A work of enduring appeal to the battlefield tourist.

9781843422624

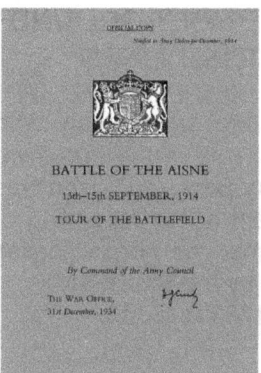

BATTLE OF THE AISNE 13TH-15TH SEPTEMBER 1914, TOUR OF THE BATTLEFIELD

Official War Office guide to the First Battle of the Aisne in September 1914 in which the BEF helped the French push the Germans across the River Aisne. The battle marked the change in the Great War between the war of movement and trench warfare.

9781845740351

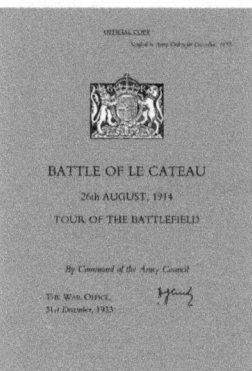

BATTLE OF LE CATEAU 26TH AUGUST 1914, TOUR OF THE BATTLEFIELD

Combined War Office map package and tour guide to Le Cateau, where the BEF stood and halted the German juggernaut for a day on August 25th 1914.

9781845740337

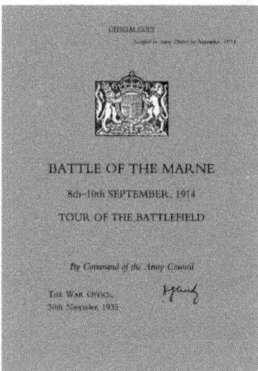

BATTLE OF THE MARNE 8TH-10TH SEPTEMBER 1914, TOUR OF THE BATTLEFIELD

The 3-day Battle of the Marne in September 1914 was the turning point of the Great War. The German capture of Paris was thwarted by the action of the French armies and the BEF. This is the official War Office guide to the battle and the battlefield.

9781845740344

YPRES: THE HOLY GROUND OF BRITISH ARMS

An important early Great War guidebook, written by a man who played a critical role in the Ypres we see today. Henry Beckles Willson was a fierce opponent of the rebuilding of Ypres, feeling that the horrific losses sustained there by the British Army.
9781783317530

naval-military-press.com

www.ingramcontent.com/pod-product-compliance
Lightning Source LLC
Chambersburg PA
CBHW071512150426
43191CB00009B/1502